INFORMATION

SYSTEMS SECURITY

INFORMATION
SYSTEMS SECURITY

ROYAL P. FISHER
IBM Corporation

PRENTICE-HALL, INC.
Englewood Cliffs, New Jersey 07632

Library of Congress Cataloging in Publication Data

Fisher, Royal P. (date)
  Information systems security.

  Includes index.
  1. Electronic data processing departments—Security
measures. 2. Computers—Access control. I. Title.
HF5548.2.F474 1984   658.4'78   83-19138
ISBN 0-13-464727-0

Editorial/production supervision: Nancy Milnamow
Jacket design: Photo Plus Art (Celine Brandes)
Cover design: Edsal Enterprises
Manufacturing buyer: Gordon Osbourne

Printed in the United States of America

10 9 8 7 6 5 4 3 2 1

ISBN 0-13-464727-0

Prentice-Hall International, Inc., *London*
Prentice-Hall of Austrialia Pty. Limited, *Sydney*
Editora Prentice-Hall do Brasil, Ltda., *Rio de Janeiro*
Prentice-Hall Canada Inc., *Toronto*
Prentice-Hall of India Private Limited, *New Delhi*
Prentice-Hall of Japan, Inc., *Tokyo*
Prentice-Hall of Southeast Asia Pte. Ltd., *Singapore*
Whitehall Books Limited, *Wellington, New Zealand*

**Dedicated to
GINGER**

CONTENTS

PREFACE

ABOUT THE BOOK

This book is probably a "first" in the industry. It was written to present a simple, effective, complete, structured approach for the design of data security in computerized systems. Equally or perhaps even more important, it provides guidance as to where attention should be focused before resources are committed to such an endeavor. That is, what cost effective actions may be taken immediately to secure information systems to an acceptable level of risk?

WHAT THE BOOK IS NOT

This book is *not* intended as an in-depth technical presentation on data security. Nor is it a treatise on specific designs for each issue within the data security framework (such as data libraries, passwords, or functional organization). Rather it has been written to present a suggested structure or methodology wherein the main issues of data security may be effectively considered. It sets forth several approaches for recognizing and handling the data security issues existing in automated information systems. And it provides a useful overview of the factors to be considered before embarking on a data security program.

WHERE TO BEGIN

What are the critical areas of control concern and what are the fundamental principles, properties, and functions of secure systems applicable in those areas? Furthermore, what is management's role and function in planning, implementing, and administering the data security function? Chapters 1 through 4 address these questions, which in the author's opinion need to be addressed *first* before resources are committed to implementing a systems methodology. Chapters 1 through 4 thereby provide a general review of good security practice in information systems.

Chapter 1: A Top Management Priority

Is data security really a matter of significance to an organization? If so, why? Is there evidence that adequate controls may be missing in today's information systems? What really needs to be done? How do I determine if a need exists in my organization for improving the level of data security? Chapter 1 points out why many existing computerized information systems lack adequate control. It offers a simple self-assessment checklist to let you rate your organization's need for management attention to prevailing data security issues and concerns.

Chapter 2: Critical Control Areas

What were the key elements to adequate control in formerly designed information systems? Where should management, audit, designers, and others interested in data security focus their attention and concentrate their resources? Chapter 2 serves as a pointer, providing direction as to where one should first look. Although the treatment is superficial (a book could be written on each area), the chapter does define the nature of each critical element and provides an understanding of the problems to be addressed.

Chapter 3: Basic Principles, Properties, and Functions

What basic principles, properties, and functions of secure systems may be used as an aid for those interested in data security? What constitutes good security practice? Chapter 3 presents a *snapshot* of the many ideas, concepts, and techniques IBM and others have found useful for developing adequate security in an information system. It quickly reviews some of the published basics of good security design. And, for those unfamiliar with data security, it provides an awareness of what is suggested practice.

Chapter 4: Management Contributions

Part 1: Management Policy, Plans and Programs. What is management's role with regard to data security? Part 1 stresses the need for management to set appropriate policy, plans, and programs for data security. Illustrations of form, content, and use are described with the referenced examples from the Appendices. Part 1 also serves to point out that data security must extend outside the information system, per se, to management in order to be effective.

Part 2: Role of the Security Administrator. Whose responsibility *is* data security? What characteristics and capabilities should a security administrator have? A function of this nature must be established in order to manage the security of the data resource. A functional matrix is suggested to aid in the affixing of the accountability. Small organizations and systems must recognize this need though they may not assign a person full-time to such a function.

THE METHODOLOGY

Many excellent articles have been published on security. To date, however, much of the information they offer remains to be synthesized into a structured and straightforward methodology. The practitioner has always needed detailed guidelines or "how to" manuals in order to perform the data security design and control function. And the auditor has searched for a simple, effective tool to assist in the adequate assessment of business controls. The methodology presented in Chapters 5 through 11 helps meet both of these basic needs. These chapters represent the main purpose of the book. They suggest the viewing of all data security concerns across eleven definable, understandable, manageable, exposure control points representing a complete data life cycle. The chapters use a methical approach to achieve the goal of presenting to management a cost-effective recommendation for system security and control.

Chapter 5: Identifying Exposures

Chapter 5 begins by defining what is meant by exposure and data security. The definitions provide a simple way of viewing the results or consequences of violations (threats) to data. Exposures may be grouped into six basic effects resulting from adverse actions: accidental/ intentional disclosure, modification, and destruction. Basic causal agents are then defined to narrow the scope of the identification process, and finally a data exposure life cycle is suggested, offering a structured thought process for identifying exposures in information systems.

Chapter 6: Exposure Control Points

Chapter 6 provides the framework within which to apply the process for identifying exposures—a data exposure life cycle comprised of eleven discrete control points.

Chapter 7: Applying the Methodology

This chapter illustrates how the structured thought process for identifying exposures can be directly applied to an information system (payroll) using the eleven-basic-exposure-control-point life cycle.

Chapter 8: Limiting Risk

How can risk be minimized? What initial steps can be taken to reduce risk? Chapter 8 offers the designer insight on how risk may be reduced, in general, in all information systems. It suggests some basic control guidelines. Such guidelines help information systems to score well (minimum exposure) when they undergo a risk analysis.

Chapter 9: Risk Analysis

Chapter 9 offers the practitioner a method for quantifying the risk associated with each defined exposure. This study may become rigorous. However, *caution* must be exercised that the process of quantification is not more costly than the expected risk. Common sense is a good guide!

Chapter 10: Basic Controls

This chapter suggests a unique way of viewing controls in order to simplify the selection process. The applicability of package software controls can be seen by viewing them across the data life cycle. Once a control is selected, its cost and its associated probability of success are assigned and recorded. Suggested worksheets are presented.

Chapter 11: Cost-Effectiveness Selection Process

Chapter 11 carries the process forward by applying the concept of return on investment (ROI) to the derived quantified values of risk and cost. Some non-cost-effective controls may be mandated by outside authority. The final adequacy of controls selected is based on a predetermined acceptable level of risk.

THE "QUIK" APPROACH

Chapter 12: "Quik" Approach

Chapter 12 offers a shortcut to the methodical approach presented in Chapters 5 through 11. The "Quik" approach uses the same methodology but reduces the rigors of quantification. It provides a *general* indication of security status rather than a detailed picture. A general assessment of controls can now be made with less effort. System weaknesses are easily identified at a higher level for control consideration. The "Quik" approach offers an excellent tool when only a fast, first-blush overview of system security is required.

SUGGESTION ON READING THIS TEXT

It is suggested by the author that this text first be read straight through for an understanding of its structure. Specific chapters or sections may then be focused on to meet individual interests and needs. Hopefully, the content will act as a catalyst for the reader to create and implement a better way, if one is to be found. The present text is just one effort among many to develop more effective approaches to data security in today's information systems.

ACKNOWLEDGEMENTS

I wish to make special acknowledgement to William H. Murray, Program Manager of Data Security, IBM Corporation, for his contribution in several chapters of this book. Many of his published basic ideas are presented as part of the overall data security framework.

In addition, I would like to express my personal gratitude to the IBM Corporation for permission to include several excerpts of IBM publications on data security. These reports, as well as several papers by other data security specialists, are included in the appendices.

I wish also to thank the following people:

- Dr. Claude W. Burill and Leon W. Ellsworth for their continued encouragement to write this book.
- Mel Quinn, manager of the Chicago Information Systems Management Institute, IBM Corporation, for his interest and encouragement in this endeavor.
- My family and other personal friends who supported me throughout the months of preparation and writing.

ROYAL P. FISHER

INFORMATION
SYSTEMS SECURITY

A TOP MANAGEMENT PRIORITY

LEVEL OF PRIORITY

Top management is entrusted with the development, growth, and prosperity of the business under its command. Its key activity has always been the planning and utilization of the organization's resources, traditionally classified as the big "M's": Men, Money, Material, and Machines-and-facilities.

With the advent of the electronic computer, a new resource has emerged for top management's concern—not the computer itself, but the elements making up the information processed by the computer. . . DATA!

Management has been slow to recognize data as a major resource. Viewed in its fragmented state, data appears to be meaningless and quite harmless. Viewed in total as an established database, however, it may constitute one of the most critical assets of the business. What gives such value to data? The answer lies in its worth to those who have it or want it. They recognize that information is power—power to manage, power to manipulate, power to control. Often the value of data is directly proportional to how much it alters or influences action or behavior.

The computer and its associated storage media enable management to have the information it wants and needs. However, management does not always assign a high priority to its responsibility in managing and protecting the *process* through which it now obtains that information.

Electronic data collection and dissemination systems are now pervasive in most organizations. Many of these systems were developed and implemented with little or no management participation and direction. Controls are not only poor but generally nonexistent. Some systems today are developed in the same manner.

Perhaps control is lacking because the data processing, audit, or other management support function has not stressed or sold the need for it. Another reason may be that computer vendors and salesmen have emphasized simplicity more than involvement. Perhaps, too, management should share some blame for its lag in really stepping up its new responsibilities in dealing with computerized information.

THE IMPETUS

Two major events have put information systems security in the foreground of management's concern. First came Equity Funding. Although publicized as a computer crime, it involved the computer only remotely in the generation of bogus policies. However, the headlines of a $27.25 million loss drew the attention of management to their responsibility for data security (i.e., the protection of information from unauthorized disclosure, modification, and/or disclosure, whether accidental or intentional). Unfortunately, lack of reinforcement and continued support of this concern made the period of recognition very brief.

The second major management awakening on data security came packaged as the Foreign Corrupt Practices Act of 1977, now known as the Business Practices and Records Act. Its provisions affect any publicly held domestic corporation. Although originally enacted by Congress to deter American companies from making improper payments to foreign officials (bribes for business), it was later enforced by rulings of the Securities and Exchange Commission (SEC) to require management to state in their financial reports that controls were adequate and functioning as intended.

The Act, with provisions amending the Securities Exchange Act of 1934, made it mandatory that a company implement a system of internal accounting controls to meet four objectives:[1]

1. Transactions are executed in accordance with management's general or specific authorization.

[1]The American Institute of Certified Public Accountants (AICPA) Statement on Auditing Standards.

2. Transactions are recorded as necessary to
    (a) permit the preparation of financial statements in conformity with generally accepted accounting principles and
    (b) maintain accountability for assets.
3. Access to assets is permitted only in accordance with management's general or specific authorization.
4. The recorded accountability for assets is compared with the existing assets at reasonable intervals and appropriate action is taken with respect to any differences.

In addition, each corporation was mandated to demonstrate upon request that it has:

1. Assessed the current status of its control system.
2. Improved any deficiencies.
3. Continued to monitor the actual effectiveness of the system.

Violation could result in a five-year prison term, a $10,000 fine, or both for the responsible executives. Once again, this made the issue of computerized information system security and control one of management's major concerns. Direct benefits from this concern were the establishment of an EDP audit function, the appointment of asset protection administrators, and the preliminary formulation of specific information system security policies, plans, and programs.

In June of 1980, however, the SEC[2] withdrew a proposal to implement the accounting provisions of the Foreign Corrupt Practices Act by requiring managers of publicly held companies to report on the adequacy of their internal controls. In withdrawing the proposal, the SEC said it would rely on voluntary management reporting . . . the fangs of the Act were pulled!

Although management has started to respond to its responsibility in managing and protecting the process through which it obtains computerized information, much still needs to be done. Chapter 4 highlights many of these activities.

Computer crime is the latest development pushing the security of information systems into headlines for management's attention. Security Pacific, the Dalton Gang, and Wells Fargo, to name a few, were well publicized. However, what is misleading here is that computer crime ap-

[2]"Taxation and Accounting," The Bureau of National Affairs Inc., Washington, D.C. 20037, page G-6, #19, 1/28/82.

pears to be the number one problem of data security. It is not! The majority of problems arise from simple errors and omissions in the data life cycle. Granted, a so-called computer caper may result in a sizable dollar loss. Until the basic accesses to the system are controlled, however, it does not make sense to concentrate on the technical or exotic aspects of system control. In other words, it is best to close the doors and windows before worrying about the cracks in the walls. Many systems today invite penetration owing to their lack of basic data security controls. The purchase of exotic and expensive hardware and software security is foolish when many basic, positive controls (such as multiple sign-offs, and the separation of duties and responsibilities) do the same job, better, for very little cost.

THE NEED

Some business organizations *are* doing an outstanding job in securing their information systems. The need remains for the majority of organizations to follow their example. This group needs a constructive approach to identify what really needs to be done beyond a "knee-jerk" reaction to the sensationalism of computer crime. Until their managers fully

- Recognize the need for setting basic data security standards and guidelines,
- Understand their role in the data security life cycle,
- Establish a formalized approach to data security, and
- Commit the resources necessary to properly administer the data security function,

the doors and windows to their information systems will remain open.

THE APPROACH

One of management's priorities today must be the establishment of data security plans, policies, and programs for the corporate environment. Also, management must be committed to participate in the design, installation, and operation of all sensitive data systems.

New management personnel assist in this management function. Several key positions are: Data Security Administrator, Data Base Administrator, Disaster Recovery Manager, EDP Auditor, and Copy Manager. In small organizations one person may wear many of these hats; even so, top management still has the responsibility for setting the overall guidelines for each function.

This book gives specific direction to managers, administrators, designers, users, and others in addressing the concerns of data security. The self-assessment checklist that follows may be used to see if any need exists in your organization for additional management awareness and involvement in data security. If you check "NO" to any of the questions presented in the checklist, that issue may be your organization's "Achilles heel." The chapters that follow will help you in identifying and understanding data security requirements.

SELF-ASSESSMENT CHECKLIST

Yes	No	How Do You Rate on Data Security?
___	___	**1.** Do you have established corporate plans, policies, programs, and guidelines for data security?
___	___	**2.** Does management really understand the terms *sensitive data, vital records, security awareness, basic controls, control center, life cycle, EDP audit, disaster/recovery,* and *adequacy of control* as applied to data processing?
___	___	**3.** If so (question 2), are each of these topics addressed by some corporate statement or directive?
___	___	**4.** Does system development use a formal management system to build the organization's information systems?
___	___	**5.** Has anyone outside of data processing evaluated the basic controls used by the information systems department? . . . periodically?
___	___	**6.** Does senior management take an active role in development and implementation of security controls?
___	___	**7.** Are auditors and security personnel involved in design changes in information systems?
___	___	**8.** Is the internal audit function supported with appropriate resources to perform its function in systems design, test, and evaluation?
___	___	**9.** Is there an established comprehensive education and training program in asset protection (data security, contingency planning, and so on)?

_____ _____ **10.** Has management established a methodology for identifying exposures, assessing risk, and approving recommended controls for those information systems now used and under current development?

_____ _____ **11.** Has there been a recent analysis to identify and prioritize all key systems/applications that are critical to the operation of the business?

_____ _____ **12.** Does your organization comply with data security guidelines as outlined by governmental bodies (for example, the SEC and its latest interpretation of the Foreign Corrupt Practices Act)?

2

CRITICAL CONTROL AREAS

Before concentrating on a methodology for designing or reviewing controls in information systems, one should focus on the key areas in a computer environment that have proved in the past to be critical to system control. Identification of a weakness in any of these areas may warrant the direction of effort there instead of toward a methodological system study. It may be far more effective to assign resources in the management and protection of these areas than to application reviews, risk analyses, or design methodologies.

This chapter is a *general* treatment of certain key factors or critical elements that need attention in every system. These elements have been the source of many problems in past systems and may well be your key to better system control. They are:

1. Adequate segregation of functions (users, owners, and servicers)
2. Authorization level at the least possible privilege
3. Centralization of change control
4. Handling of reject/reentry
5. Control of manual interfaces
6. Maintenance of tape/disk libraries
7. Establishment of security awareness (physical, data)
8. Disaster/recovery planning

9. Instigation of a vital records program
10. Test/production program library control
11. Evaluation of operations/user satisfaction
12. Utilization of software utilities and aids
13. Definition of a system development methodology (standards)
14. Provision of training/retraining programs
15. Monitoring of personnel (systems programmer, DBA, DP manager, auditor)
16. Identification of inventories (data/users)
17. Development of policies/contracts
18. Formalization of I/O control

This list, although certainly not complete, highlights the majority of opportunity areas for improving control in today's DP systems. A concerned management should review these critical control areas before committing resources to a specific data security project. A beginning EDP auditor would do well to first concentrate on these points before becoming involved with the programmed applications in DP systems. A systems designer should view this list as an aid to awareness of potential problem areas needing control. Each of these critical areas is described briefly below.

1. Adequate Segregation of Functions

This key factor ensures that adequate separation of duties and responsibilities exists in present systems and is designed into new systems. In particular, it addresses the authority, responsibility, and involvement of DP personnel. For example, no programmer should be involved with the user's application program. (This topic is discussed in Chapter 3 in the section on "Basic Principles.")

If possible, each of the following functions should be performed by a separate person. Although in small organizations this is not feasible, one must recognize the possible danger as an individual assumes more than one of these functions:

- Application design
- Application programming
- Database administration
- Data entry

- Library management
- Maintenance programming
- Management
- Operation—job initiation
- Operation—data input activity
- Operation—data output activity
- Output distribution
- Program testing
- Scheduling
- System library maintenance
- Systems programming
- Other management and control areas

An organizational chart or grid that plots personnel vs. function is an excellent tool to determine the extent of such separation.

2. Authorization Level at the Least Possible Privilege

In order to maintain the highest level of system security and integrity, each user of the system should be authorized no more privileges than absolutely necessary. Rather than encourage additional use through lack of restrictions, the system should grant each user only the minimum privileges needed in the performance of his or her assigned job.

A study should be conducted (whether in existing systems or those under design) as to the privileges granted each user. An effective test method is to answer the following basic question: "If this particular report were no longer available, or access to a certain file were closed to the user, could the user still perform his or her *assigned* job?" One must think through what is the minimum system privilege each user *needs*— not wants!

3. Centralization of Change Control

This factor is critical to all systems. Although a system may be designed with the highest degree of data integrity and control, this protection will be defeated by a failure to control any or all changes to that system.

Each DP organization should have an established change control group. In a small organization with few applications this group may be only one person. The group's primary function is to provide independent checks and balances on *all* suggested and approved changes to the system. They review all requests for stated purpose, need, cost, impact, and authorization. This group may also control the use of all system penetration tools and utilities such as SUPERZAP. SUPERZAP is an IBM software program that permits change to an operating system program at machine-code or object-code level. Such changes are quick and generally unrecorded. Although SUPERZAP is an effective tool for maintaining higher production levels, it does present a security control problem. IBM today recommends the use of its System Modification Program (SMP), where possible, since it offers control over whatever changes are made. Control of such tools as SUPERZAP by a change control group strengthens the total system's accountability and auditability properties.

Most problems reported today in change control are the result of "quick fixes." Many quick fixes use computer software tools to break into a system, bypass the problem (or attempt to correct it), and patch a continuation linkage between the two segments. Temporary unauthorized code inserted at this time may go unnoticed and remain a permanent part of the program.

A quick fix often occurs because a problem arises at an inopportune time. For example, after a system conversion, the third-shift operator experiences a problem at 2 A.M. Rather than disturb management at that hour, the operator attempts a quick fix. Although the operator's motives and intentions are admirable, the security of the system has been broken and its integrity is now questionable. All tools and procedures for quick fixes need to be controlled!

4. Handling of Reject/Reentry

Although a system may not be changed, the need still exists for handling and controlling data that is rejected and/or reentered. In past systems this area has been a favorite spot for theft to occur. For example, an employee who works in data entry for a large department store can simply spindle, mutilate, and miscode his or her personal purchase input documents, causing rejections. The employee then discards the rejected documents.

A separate control function is needed in all systems to provide for the proper handling and disposition of all rejects and reentries.

5. Control of Manual Interfaces

Every point in a system where man interfaces with machine (where a resource passes from one person's control to another's) is a critical point for control. This includes not only DP operations but external points such as terminal entry as well.

First, a control check should be made of the physical environment. Is the machine in a secure area? What precautions exist to protect the machine from acts of God and humans? Needed next is a study of the personal interfaces. Who are the users? Are they trained, qualified, responsible people?

A review of user procedures with direct observation of user performance often points out weaknesses. For example, the password entry is not masked; messages are retained on the video display unit (CRT) unless erased by the user; passwords are taped or printed on the console; the system is open to be played with by anyone (including the janitor) during user's absence; and user input repeatedly "locks" the system (renders it inoperable until released by an appropriately assigned control mechanism) owing to entry mistakes.

The external controls at any data entry point are just as critical as the system's internal safeguards. It is the combination of controls both internally and externally that determines the actual degree of system protection. The designer and auditor should review both types of control not only for security purposes but also for sources of error and inefficiency.

An area of great concern for security today is the interface of word processing to the main computer system. Although the main system may have excellent controls, the tieing in of word processing presents the opportunity for system penetration. For example, many such tie-ins are done on a test basis that allows circumvention of existing controls in order to facilitate integration. Investigations have indicated that this occurrence is generally a case of management oversight.

6. Maintenance of Tape/Disk Libraries

Tapes and disks (magnetic media) in most organizations today represent the information resource upon which the business functions. If the information resource were lost or modified, the business might not survive.

Just as banks must account for every dollar in their inventory, an organization must have controls to account for every item in its information library. Inspections and examinations of library documentation, procedures, operations, and even personnel are mandatory. Every library item and its activity needs to be logged and checked for availability, accuracy, usage, and maintenance. Far too many organizations today have library files openly available to users, programmers, and operators. In fact, many organizations have multiple libraries whose existence is unknown. Division, branch, and plant site locations may have minicomputers that fostered the development of independent libraries not reported to the main site location.

7. Establishment of Security Awareness

Security is everyone's job! Many organizations, however, emphasize or give training in security only during new-hire orientation. As the employee continues to work, there is no reinforcement of that initial assignment of responsibility.

Each organization should have a security awareness program that reviews and emphasizes the continued security responsibility of each employee. Effective techniques include film sessions, staff meetings, and customized forms such as IBM's Security Assessment Questionnaire (see Appendix A and the discussion in Chapter 4.) The importance of security may be emphasized by policy statements such as IBM's original 2-109A and current corporate instruction CI-104, which state that "fulfillment of DP asset protection responsibilities must be mandatory, and should be considered a condition of continued employment." Furthermore, an annual, signed certification by the employee that he or she has read and understood the company's published "Asset Protection Guidelines" and "Data Security Guidelines" reinforces the organization's level of security awareness.

The section on "Risk Assessment Program" in Chapter 4 offers more insight into this program and the use of a security assessment questionnaire.

8. Disaster/Recovery Planning

The purpose of disaster/recovery planning is to take steps in advance to ensure continuity of business information if the DP capability is lost. A *disaster* is defined as the loss of DP capability (to whatever extent). *Recovery plans* are measures to be taken to restore the business on a near-normal-as-possible basis. Disaster encompasses far more than major catastrophes such as earthquakes, tornadoes, or floods. The focus in disaster/recovery planning should be on recognition of emergency conditions and implementation of planned processes for returning the business to a normal operating mode as soon as possible. Any event that causes a loss of DP capability (such as personal illness) qualifies as a disaster. Therefore, the extent and severity of possible disasters vary widely. Chapter 4 describes the type of plans and planning effort required to develop a total disaster/recovery plan.

Planning effort and responsibility is an organization undertaking. That is, not only DP but also management, users, and other affected parties participate in the program. In the event of loss of DP capability, users are responsible for the continuity of their business function until DP meets its responsibility to restore processing capability. This is a key element of disaster recovery planning.

A plan by itself is incomplete. Each plan needs to be tested and action taken to correct the discovered inadequacies. In other words, this is a continual planning *process*, where the process is even more important than the plan itself. It is the process that affords understanding and readiness.

All organizations should have an up-to-date, tested, organizational disaster recovery plan. The end product, first and foremost, is not a paper document but a tested, proven capability to recover. Testing is the vehicle that changes disaster recovery planning from a concept into a reality.

9. Instigation of a Vital Records Program

In order to protect the most valuable data assets in an organization, the data resources (tapes, disks, diskettes, cards, and so on) must be classified, and each must be assigned to a level of business need. The following four basic classifications may be used:

Vital records. The loss of these records could terminate the business. Their information often is irreplaceable and is needed immediately for the business to function. Examples might include key programs, master records and files, operational documentation, disaster recovery plans, and certain input/output data.

Essential records. The loss of this information would certainly disrupt the operation of the business. Although the business might survive, the level of operation and productivity would be seriously affected. These records can be reproduced, but generally extra expense, time, and effort are called for. Examples might include secondary programs, operational logs, and business histories.

Important records.   The loss of these records causes inconvenience but rarely disruption of operation. Usually they are readily replaceable. Examples might include general systems documentation, special programs, and procedures for testing old applications and future system prototype data.

Useful records.   The loss of these records creates nary a ripple in the operation of the business. They are often viewed as nonessential and may be found to be no longer necessary. They are nice to have, but their absence creates no problems. Examples include various management, user, and data processing reports.

If desired, vital records may be further subclassified. Such breakdowns may or may not provide additional benefit.

The key to a *vital records program* is the recognition of the data that is necessary to the survival of the business—the vital records. Controls, safeguards, and tested plans are mandatory. This program includes a tested disaster recovery plan and all related backup plans. See Chapter 4 for further discussion.

10. Test/Production Program Library Control

The control of test libraries and test programs from production libraries and production programs is key to a system's integrity and security. *Production* is defined as those applications and systems that have been tested, approved, and made part of the actual operation of the business.

The promotion of any new program to operational status needs very careful control. IBM's Advanced Administrative System utilizes eight basic steps:[1]

Step 1.   The programmer writes the new program, then signs and submits a Promotion Sheet.

Step 2.   The Promotion Sheet is reviewed; the program is inspected for integrity and then signed by the programmer's manager.

---

[1]See James Martin, *Security, Accuracy and Privacy in Computer Systems,*(Englewood Cliffs, N.J.: Prentice-Hall, Inc., 1973), p. 389.

Step 3.   A central test group passes the program through all phases of testing and then certifies by signature that all standards were met.

Step 4.   The applications control group inspects and reviews the program from the viewpoint of total systems impact and approves the tested program for movement to the "live" program residence file.

Step 5.   The systems operation group, only with the authorization of the application control group, runs a utility program that moves the new program to the "live" program file. This utility program produces a record of all programs moved to the system residence file.

Step 6.   An on-line control group, concerned with system performance and reliability, exercises the program in the "live" system in a controlled manner to minimize risk of system performance degradation and program malfunction.

Step 7.   A functional group to whom the program relates (e.g., payroll) checks the operation of the program to verify that it does what is wanted.

Step 8.   A terminal user test is undertaken to ensure operational satisfaction, positive man-machine interaction, and security from operator misuse. If all steps pass and are signed off, the new program becomes operational.

Although smaller systems may require fewer people, all organizations need a formalized control procedure for moving any new program into "live" business production.

11. Evaluation of Operations/User Satisfaction

What is sought is a complete understanding by both operations and the user of what each contributes and receives in return. Meetings are scheduled where they exchange viewpoints. Satisfaction is then developed from mutual understanding and agreement.

Most problems in operations/user satisfaction occur as a result of inadequate communications and contact between parties. Both the user and operations may have learned to live with poor or unnecessarily expensive computer processing, unreasonable overtime, month-end cutoff problems, and disgruntled employees. What is needed is a meeting of the minds. Sometimes a third party may be able to serve as a communications link in uncovering and resolving differences of opinion (about contributions, responsibilities, expectations). Interviews offer the opportunity for a third party to uncover problems and present both sides of the issue in an understandable form.

Another approach to consider may be the use of a DP-user satisfaction reporting system as developed by Mathews & Company.[2] According to firms using this system, called, "How're We Doing?", it offers a good management tool for facilitating communication between data processing and the users it services. It requires users, during the course of a month, to make notation on a log if there is a problem with data processing for any of nine performance-related criteria: timeliness of output, accuracy of output, distribution of output, quality of output, on-line availability, response time, systems development schedules, response to problems, and attitude and cooperativeness. Such a system offers two advantages: (1) direct feedback of user satisfaction, and (2) a vehicle for DP to discuss and resolve common problems between parties.

A study of user satisfaction often presents the opportunity for a dramatic increase in morale, productivity, and user involvement.

12. Utilization of Software Utilities and Aids

Software tools are available to systems programmers that provide direct changes to production programs at object-code or machine level. Needless to say, such powerful utility programs must be controlled. These utilities (of which "Superzap" is probably the most common) should be catalogued, issued only by authorization, and monitored in use. They must be immediately available yet tightly controlled.

All utilities that add, delete, modify, and copy data should be under controlled supervision. The indiscriminate use of such utilities could foster the availability of information for personal gain or revenge.

A data dictionary or directory is a tool for the management and control of data. The *dictionary* contains data definitions and the *directory* shows where the data is used. These are excellent audit aids for identifying and tracing the availability of data to the system and its users. It is imperative that all database systems maintain an up-to-date data dictionary. This is generally the responsibility of the database administrator. This function, therefore, requires set control procedures for operation and maintenance.

[2]"Report Card System Gauges Satisfaction of DP Users," *Management Information Systems Week*, July 28, 1982.

13. Definition of a System Development Methodology

At any given time, several application program projects may be under concurrent development. Each project may have separate project leaders and programs for development. For example, John may develop system A using evolutionary structuring while Joe develops system B using hierarchial monolithic structuring. Although both will work independently, their integration and maintenance presents costly problems. In order to achieve consistency in systems as to standards and procedures, an overall project development methodology is necessary. Every organization should have a defined methodology, framework, or structure as a basis for the design of DP systems. Such a methodology allows the development of compatible, auditable, maintainable systems for minimum cost.

14. Provision of Training/Retraining Programs

The majority of problems in data processing systems are due to human error and omission. The cause is directly traceable to inadequate training or retraining.

Each organization should periodically review the training facilities offered to personnel for effective and efficient performance on assigned jobs. In particular, the new programming systems under design and development often require new methods for handling the physical operation of the system. Trial and error is not a good teacher!

The human resource will only do right things at the right time if trained to do so. Any system can be no better than the people who work with it. Sizable increases in productivity and reduction of errors can be realized through the availability of qualified training programs.

15. Monitoring of Personnel

Data may be threatened by exposure to several key DP management positions. Systems programmers pose grave risks with their capability of making changes on a machine-level basis. Such changes may never be recognized by others.

There is no perfect safeguard from a systems programmer. Work may be assigned such that no systems programmer works alone. This arrangement forces collusion in order for a threat to occur. However, dual controls are expensive, and many installations have no need for two such people. Background checks, references, and even lie detector tests have been administered by some organizations to reduce this exposure. Several organizations have bonded these employees to protect the business against massive loss.

A logical approach is to pay them well, keep them busy in the care and feeding of the operating system, ban them from application programs, and utilize structured walkthroughs or inspections for departmental review of their work.

Data processing positions such as DP manager, database administrator, and systems manager offer opportunities to enter a system undetected. Most computer systems are appallingly vulnerable to their own staff. The understanding and use of basic principles, properties, and functions as presented in Chapter 3 can greatly alleviate, if not eradicate, this concern. The unchallenged auditor may also prove to be a risk exposure to the whole system.

16. Identification of Inventories

Many DP organizations have no actual physical record of *all* the data assets residing in their shop. Worse yet, many have no record as to where they are located.

Each program, utility, routine, software package, and the like that belongs to the organization should be accounted for. The tape/disk library is the repository. Copies of unique routines developed by programmers must be declared company property and properly controlled. Many such routines reside with the programmer who developed them, locked in personal drawers and viewed as his or her personal property.

No degree of protection can ever be assured if the data inventory is not totally defined!

17. Development of Policies/Contracts

This factor keys in on the management aspect of data processing systems. Although a system may be designed technically perfect, its administration may render useless the benefits derived from implementation.

Management must state its policy with respect to the protection of DP assets. Such policy and practice may take a form such as presented in Appendix B, which is a sample of IBM's "Guidelines for DP Asset Protection." It is the management policy that sets the standards, practices, and responsibilities for all parties involved in DP systems. Without this "guide" the organization has no measurement and control of its DP systems.

Contracts that bind the organization's personnel to selected services should all be reviewed by legal and audit. Often what is *not* said is what the organization inferred was offered. Data processing will be involved in contracts for hardware, software, service centers, consulting, programming, time sharing, and insurance, to name a few. All of these need to have their stated provisions monitored and reviewed.

18. Formalization of I/O Control

All systems must have some type of formalized control over input and output. An I/O control group is an excellent repository for receiving, transferring, and monitoring all input/output data. One major responsibility of this group is data integrity.

The adage "garbage in, garbage out" is a warning against garbage input. The majority of all garbage in a system enters through the original input. The I/O control group is the key to control of input as well as output. They interface between the user departments and computer operations people. Their primary control tests are accuracy checks, validity checks, reasonableness checks, verification and completeness checks.

Realtime systems may require more than one I/O control section to handle terminal entry from remote locations. The group at each site may be only one person. The emphasis here is that such a group exists and interfaces with all data systems!

The eighteen critical elements just described have proved to be the most troublesome spots in DP systems for data security and control. All new systems should address these issues in the design stage. Audit must check to see that they have been considered. And management should first focus its concern for data security on these key areas.

3

PRINCIPLES, PROPERTIES, AND FUNCTIONS

Data security is the protection of data from unauthorized disclosure, modification, and/or destruction whether accidental or intentional. It is beneficial to develop an understanding of the fundamentals of data security before planning, designing, or reviewing any information system. This chapter provides an overview of these fundamentals.[1]

BASIC PRINCIPLES

A cardinal principle of the accounting profession calls for "the adequate separation of duties and responsibilities." In data processing, any unreasonable opportunity for the inclusion of errors or the dishonest conduct of employees necessitates the application of this principle. Other principles, as discussed below, further support this basic one.

1. Segregation of Duties—Multiple People

Segregation of duties means separating the activities of a process among several people. For example, in data processing, the data entry operator should not also have the responsibility for verifying that data.

[1]For detailed discussion, see IBM Publication G320-5649, "Data Security Control and Procedures—A Philosophy for DP Installations," 2d ed., March 1977, pp. 2–6.

A programmer should not maintain his own code. A system designer should not be allowed to access application modules.

When this principle is applied, transposition errors will be more readily caught before entering the system. And a user may discover an attempt by the designer to access control over his system. Collusion also may be required in order for a breach of security to occur; that is, more than one person is needed to break security, and the capability of detection is thereby enhanced. Quality assurance, systems review, or even maintenance may then have the opportunity of uncovering an authorized programmed routine (often referred to as the Bomb, Trojan Horse, or the like) planted in the program by the programmer.

2. No Access to Sensitive Combinations of Resources

Sensitive information is data that, if exposed, could influence the posture of a given business situation. As pointed out in Chapter 8, information by itself may lack significance, but combinations of such information may become sensitive.

For example, a programmer may not be authorized to view employee salaries. However, the same programmer may have access to personnel location and statistical data. If so, by inquiring first, "What is the employee's address?" and second, "How many employees at that *specific* address earn more than $20,000, $25,000, $30,000, . . . ?" the programmer can attempt to focus in on any employee's salary. Such combinations of resource information may be very subtle and require careful study to identify.

Sensitive combinations more often include data and an associated asset. For instance, individuals who have access to both the primary asset and the control data governing it, such as inventory control data and inventory, present a definite security risk. The pilfering of funds at Union Dime Bank is an example. Union Dime Bank had a teller who not only controlled a primary asset (dormant accounts) but also controlled all data governing that asset (debits, credits, balances, and so on). The teller took advantage of the situation and maneuvered money in and out of the accounts to cover his betting losses at the racetrack.

3. Prohibit Conversion and Concealment

Employees should not be placed in a tempting position where they could convert and conceal assets for their own benefit. A common violation of this principle is the assignment of a single computer operator to the third shift. Long production runs with few operating procedures might appear to justify a single operator. After some time, however, the operator, out of boredom or need, might begin to make and sell copies of the production run output or might secretly develop a service bureau business paid for unknowingly by the employer. Even worse, the employee might print or copy available data files (customers, commissions, and so on) and sell them to competitors.

The greatest opportunities for conversion and concealment of data, however, may not lie within the data processing production shop but rather occur outside it, where input/output communication with the data base is possible.

Information systems that have been designed with inadequate separation of duties and responsibilities and/or allow access to combinations of sensitive resources are ripe for a conversion-and-concealment violation. It is not the use of a computer or a computerized data base that creates this opportunity; it is the inadequate use of the control capabilities available. In fact, a computer and its data base can afford better control over a business than the manual system that they replace. Control is achieved through proper planning, design, testing, utilization, and management of the many control features available in today's computer systems.

4. Individual Cannot Both Originate and Approve Transactions

In order to improve efficiency and speed of operations, it may be deemed reasonable to combine the process of origination and approval of transactions. However, even though this responsibility is entrusted to a long-term, highly respected, honest employee with an impeccable work record, such absolute control violates acceptable accounting practice.

Ms. X, for example, was a trusted 25-year bank employee, the recipient of many awards, looked upon as a "pillar" of that local bank. Unknown to the bank, Ms. X made gifts of money totaling $1.2 million to the poor and destitute. She considered it a Christian deed, an act of divine guidance. When she was finally caught, however, the bank considered it outright stealing, a criminal act of robbery. Nevertheless, the situation proved so embarrassing to the bank that charges were dropped upon her dismissal.

Most organizations require that those whose duty it is to originate sensitive transactions are subject to independent approval. However, they often fail to insure that authorized approvers cannot also originate.

All businesses need a system of checks and balances. If one could approve his own expense accounts, one might expend limitless funds.

SYSTEM PROPERTIES

To help ensure an acceptable level of risk, a system should manifest the following properties:

1. Integrity

A system should do only what it is supposed to do and nothing else. It performs according to a planned set of specifications—even when it fails. It possesses the essentials of wholeness or completeness. Such a system has *integrity.*

For example, a timer on a bank vault door will activate opening at only a preset time and no other; a read-only data set will refuse all attempts at change from any source; a check will be dispensed only to the proper individual at the right time for the right amount.

The test of integrity is predictability. If, for every stimulus to the system, the response can be predicted both when the system is performing properly and when it is failing, it has integrity.

By way of illustration, Figure 3.1 indicates that a system with integrity, when met with an abnormal stimulus, is still predictable in its performance. The property of integrity provides the capability to respond

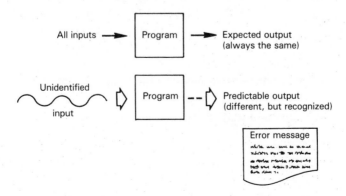

Figure 3.1

with corrective action. Such a system greatly reduces the potential for information exposure and thus raises the level of data security.

2. Auditability

A system that is *auditable* allows an independent reviewer to verify its activity with relative ease at any time. The system must *demonstrate* that it is performing to specifications, complying with control requests, being used as intended, and conforming with standards of good practice. In order to meet this criterion, the system should be constructed entirely of auditable components. It needs to be modular in design, each module capable of communicating with others only across a limited number of formally defined interfaces. Such a system therefore has the ability to record all the transactions (i.e., requests, events, contents, stimuli, responses) at the interfaces.

A test of auditability is *accountability*. A system should be able to fix responsibility for every significant event at the level of a single individual. It should be able to point to some "one" or some "party" as accountable for any system action. Such a system would be capable of holding any person accessing that system completely accountable for his actions.

Such a system must also have *visibility*. That is, variances from expected behavior, use, or content must come to the attention of management in such a way as to permit timely and appropriate corrective action.

3. Controllability

A system that possesses *controllability* permits management to exercise a directing or restraining influence over its use, behavior, or content. This property limits the capability of a system to pass other than intended or prescribed resources between domains (i.e., work areas or spheres of influence).[1] For example, I may be able to submit charges for legitimate business expenses but not be able to approve, issue, or redirect the payment of funds. Furthermore, I may be allowed to submit expenses only for particular types of charges associated with my department.

In order to achieve such a control posture, each auditable module must be individually controllable. This implies that each module control

---

[1]See the section entitled "Control domains" in Chapter 8.

its own domain, so that it passes to other modules *only* those actions intended.

A test of controllability is *granularity*. Granularity requires that the size of the module to be controlled is small enough to constitute an acceptable level of risk. For example, if a payroll module includes the functions of requesting, authorizing, and making payments, it fails granularity.

No one module should control a resource of such size that it can materially affect the continuance of the business. It is a management responsibility to set the level of risk (or influence) acceptable at each interface.

SYSTEM FUNCTIONS

A strategy for achieving the properties of integrity, auditability, and controllability is to place functional controls at each domain's interface. These controls protect the passage of information in the system from being compromised. They represent the system designer's greatest contribution in achieving maximum data security.

The functions are best described in the sequence in which they are designed into a system.

1. Identification

The *identification* function allows us to establish identifier (names, code symbols) tor each system user and resource. Its purpose is to afford evidence of reality. In other words, this function identifies by some acceptable means the people, hardware, software and other resources available to a system.

Identification implies only that a record exists in the system that associates an identifier with a defined user or resource. A claim to some identity has been established at this point. For example, employee John Jones; data record PYRL; terminal T1.

The identifier should be as concise as possible; yet large enough to uniquely name all information associable with that identification. For example, in place of entering a name, address, or title to identify a person, an employee-number or account-number code is sufficient. Furthermore, for purposes of individual accountability in a system, the more specific the identifier the better. Generally, the user population and nature of the business dictate the appropriate identifier selected.

2. Authentication

The *authentication* function is the act of collecting evidence to an acceptable level of risk that the claim of identity is valid. Simply stated, it is acceptable validation of identity. It provides the capability to verify the identified user or resource. This may be accomplished by comparing something that this individual knows, has, is, or can do to a recorded reference. For example:

- *Something he knows—Password.* A secret coded word known only to the user and the system.
- *Something he has—Photo identification card.* A picture of the individual that may be matched to the person presenting the card.
- *Something he is—Physical appearance.* A bodily comparison of appearance to memory on a face-to-face basis.
- *Something he can do—Signature.* A unique but reproducible behavior such as the manner in which the name is written.

Authentication, therefore, normally relies on some "thing" that only one entity knows (e.g., key word, procedure), has (e.g., token, key), is (e.g., hand geometry, lip prints) or can do (e.g., speech, stunt). For instance, when children are transported alone by airplane to their relatives, only the stewardess *knows* the name of their dog or teddybear. The children are not released into the custody of others until the so-called relative volunteers the name. The use of a password in a system acts in much the same way.

In addition, the authentication of the *source* of data in an information system is key to data security. It helps determine how much trust can be placed in the accuracy, reliability, and completeness of the information presented by that system.

3. Authorization

The *authorization* function's sole purpose is to state who is allowed to do what to a given resource. This function generally relates a user with a resource through defined rules of authorization. That is, authorization establishes rules that restrict system users to exercising only predefined actions to the data resource. Each individual must first have explicit authorization by management for access to the data resource. This function can then be easily administered through an authorization table. The authorization table illustrated in Figure 3.2 is one example.

User Authorization Table

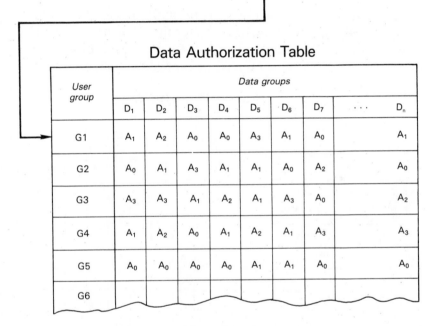

User ID	Terminal ID	Security code	User group
012471	T4	SVLP	G1
611282	T1	FSBB	G2
151124	T8	KDFF	G6
567112	T1	KYSS	G2
400277	T1	GGHM	G3

Types of Authorization

A_0: No permission
A_1: Read record
A_2: Read, update record
A_3: Read, update, create or delete record

Data Authorization Table

User group	Data groups								
	D_1	D_2	D_3	D_4	D_5	D_6	D_7	...	D_n
G1	A_1	A_2	A_0	A_0	A_3	A_1	A_0		A_1
G2	A_0	A_1	A_3	A_1	A_1	A_0	A_2		A_0
G3	A_3	A_3	A_1	A_2	A_1	A_3	A_0		A_2
G4	A_1	A_2	A_0	A_1	A_2	A_1	A_3		A_3
G5	A_0	A_0	A_0	A_0	A_1	A_1	A_0		A_0
G6									

Figure 3.2

The authorization table in Figure 3.2 provides a series of steps for proper identification, authentication, and then authorization to a specifically predefined set of data. For example, employee number 012471 identifies himself on terminal T4. This system authenticates the user by the matching of a security code (SVLP) and existence in reported user group (G1). The employee is then authorized to perform only those actions (A_0 through A_3) stated in the data authorization table. He may only read a record in data group 1 and is prohibited from any action in data groups 3, 4, 7.

An additional matrix control grid, shown in Figure 3.3, is often beneficial to a system. This grid identifies the user, and then, before any further activity takes place, checks on both the need and capability (training) of that user to access specific data. Although a payroll clerk may need access to a payroll record, the clerk must first possess the necessary capability in use of the terminal before attempting an entry. This preliminary screening helps prevent inexperienced users from disrupting the system. In Figure 3.3, the first user is prevented from performing two types of transactions until he has proven skill to do so.

4. Delegation

In order to maintain and apply the authorization function, *delegation* is necessary. Delegation provides for the origination, recording, and maintenance of the access rules. This function determines who, under what circumstances, may exercise or change the rules of authorization.

Authorization Table

HOLD!

	Need to know? Adequate training?	Transaction types									
User ID	Need			X		X		X			
	Capability			X		☼ (HOLD!)					
User ID	Need		X			X		X			
	Capability		X			X		X			

Figure 3.3

In small systems this task may be accomplished by the security administrator. Large systems that have a complex structure of users, resources, locations, and activities may require a sophisticated delegation mechanism that allows management to update the rules in a realtime mode. Needless to say, such a mechanism needs to be controlled.

As an example, IBM's software access control package "RACF" (Resource Allocation and Control Facility) provides extensive delegation functions. Group administrators and data set owners can be assigned and changed, and they can control other users' access to their groups and data sets. Like other controls in a formal organization, functional control is delegated downward.

In a stricter sense, several systems marketed today are designed so only the designated control operator can be delegated the authority to change operation IDs and passwords. Such is the case with IBM's 3790 system.

5. Journaling

After identification, authentication, authorization, and delegation, the next step is the *journaling* of all meaningful activity that takes place. Journals provide written records of the use of the system's resources. They offer three major benefits:

1. Providing for reconstruction, backup/recovery.
2. Fixing accountability—trace and identify.
3. Gaining visibility—see what is happening.

Systems should never be designed without a journaling capability (i.e., capturing who did what, where, why, when, and how). Journaling is the most effective way to monitor adherence to company policies, objectives, rules, and standards of performance. Generally, any point where a significant resource or accountability passes from one person's control to another's (see the section entitled "Control domains" in Chapter 8) is a key area for audit-trail considerations.

Audit trails (journals, logs), no matter how complete, are ineffective without the next function, surveillance.

6. Surveillance

Someone needs to review the journals. Someone needs to monitor the activity for variance from the expected behavior, use, or content.

This is the *surveillance* function. Not only must the system journals be reviewed, but appropriate *action* must follow. Management must be informed of irregular activity or any unexpected system behavior. If warranted, management can take immediate, positive, corrective action.

For example, the absence of the surveillance function in a major bank's night depository system resulted in a $37,000 loss within one hour. Here is what happened:

One evening, an ingenious individual donned a guard's uniform and drove to a branch bank located in a large shopping mall shortly after the bank had closed. He stood in front of the night depository drawer and held a bag with a sign saying, "Depository broken, Place all deposits in bag." As the various shop owners closed for the night, they dutifully placed their store receipts into the bag. The guard then folded his bag and drove off into the sunset.

Surveillance requires both internal and external system mechanisms. Once a variance is detected, the security system can immediately initiate a preplanned action such as a terminal lockup. Corporate management must still be informed of any irregularities to decide what additional corrective measures, if any, are most appropriate.

These six basic functions are probably the most important considerations in designing adequate security controls for the data resource!

4

MANAGEMENT CONTRIBUTIONS

PART I: MANAGEMENT POLICY, PLANS AND PROGRAMS

One of the most critical parts of data security is management's participation and commitment. Unless management establishes plans, programs, and policies, data security is just two words, purely lip service. This chapter defines and illustrates the role management must play in the security of information systems. Keep in mind that the following are corporate plans, not data processing plans, although DP may certainly be involved in or affected by them. They help management assess and evaluate the level of security throughout the organization.

THE POLICY

A corporate data security *policy* establishes the security responsibilities for the generation, handling, servicing, and using of business information. Such a policy must be supported by documented guidelines, procedures, and/or standards, which it is management's responsibility to formulate. For example, specific statements must be made with respect to the responsibilities of the owner, user, custodian, and manager of data. Appendix B, "Guidelines for DP Asset Protection," presents a sample of such policy statements and supportive guidelines as established by the IBM Corporation. Paragraph B1, page 5 of the IBM Guidelines, formally states top management's position or policy with regard to protecting the company's information assets: "Fulfillment of DP asset protection responsibilities must be mandatory, and should be considered a *condition of continued employment*." Paragraphs B2, B3, B4, and B5 then outline the responsibilities of those who come in contact with the data asset.

Managers are quite recognizable by virtue of position and assignment. However, a most worthwhile exercise is the determination of the user, custodian, and owner. Usually they are not the same individuals. Furthermore, ownership is often claimed by many and recognized by few. A simple, effective tool that may be used in this determination is a *data grid*, which makes use of the documentation of data inventory. If no such document exists, then the first action is to locate, describe, and define the existing data inventory. This may be in a variety of forms (data sets, cards, reports, tapes, disks, diskettes, paper, and so on). Then a grid such as shown in Table 4.1 can be constructed, debated, and completed by the parties involved. Accountability to a recognizable, per-

TABLE 4.1 Data Inventory Accountability

Data Item	Owner[a]	Custodian[b]	User[c]
1	J. Brown[d]	M. Sharp	D. Green, T. Smith, L. Kline
2	A. Smith	M. Sharp	T. Pai, A. Krull, R. Van Loon
3	P. Jones	T. Rogers	T. Watson
4	M. Kline	M. Sharp	D. Brown, E. Zayer, R. Fisher

[a]*Owner:* The responsible employee or agent assigned to make and communicate certain judgments and decisions regarding a data asset's value, importance, classification, access, custody, security, and control.

[b]*Custodian:* The responsible employee or agent having authorized possession of the data asset. Custodians are assigned total responsibility for business control and protection of all data assets while in their custody.

[c]*User:* The responsible employee or agent authorized to access the data asset. Users are totally responsible and accountable for the disposition of all data made available by their request or personal action.

[d]A department or office may also be included.

sonal level is now achieved, and information can be managed and controlled.

Notice in Appendix D, "Corporate Data Security Policy—The Hartford," paragraphs II.B and II.C. Emphasis here is placed on identifying data owners and custodians for establishing adequate control on the data asset. Paragraphs I.A through I.D officially state the corporate policy.

The Department of Social Services (see Appendix E) also offers an overall directional statement for the Health and Welfare Agency Data Center. The responsibility for data security as shared by the data center and the user is described in the directional statement.

It is mandatory that some corporate policy of the types just mentioned be formally stated for use as a basis of information security or even general security throughout the organization. Lack of such a policy has been a prime reason for improper use and care of company information.

MANAGER'S POLICY

Managers of an organization require policy statements regarding their activity and responsibility to the data assets of the business. Such statements are generally presented in very broad terms (overall asset protection) to encompass any assets of value to the organization. Some typical policy statements are:

- The protection of assets such as employees, physical property, and information relating to the conduct of business is a basic management responsibility.
- Managers are responsible for identifying and protecting all assets within their assigned area of management control.
- They will assign asset ownership, responsibility, and accountability to proper personnel under their supervision.
- They are responsible for ensuring that all employees understand their obligation to protect company assets.
- They are responsible for implementing security practices and procedures that are consistent with generally accepted practice (or some specific statement or practice such as company security manual or manager's manual) and with the value of the asset.
- Finally, managers are responsible for noting variance from established security practice and for initiating corrective action.

By itself, a corporate information policy is not enough! It represents only an official statement of position taken by corporate management. The policy statement must be supported with plans and programs for executing all actions necessary to safeguard the data assets. Several key management plans and programs[1] of particular interest are listed below:

Plans
- Vital Records Plan
- Access Control Plan
- Emergency Response Plan
- Interim Processing Plan
- Restoration Plan

Programs
- Data Classification Program
- Risk Assessment Program

Collectively these constitute an asset protection program that is an integral part of, or directly related to, a disaster/recovery plan. THESE PLANS AND PROGRAMS MAY HAVE NOTHING OR EVERYTHING TO DO WITH DATA PROCESSING (i.e., they are essential in every business with or without a computer installation; they are simply good business practices.) In some form they are generally already in place, to some degree!

Most organizations may identify these plans and programs under different headings. In any event, they comprise the basic core of planned activity necessary to conduct the business on a continual "normal" basis. Unfortunately, in many organizations that profess to have them they prove upon examination to be any or all of the following:

- Incomplete
- Inaccurate
- Insufficient
- Infeasible
- Missing
- Misunderstood
- Out of date
- Not tested

[1]IBM Publication G320-5649, "Data Security Controls and Procedures—A Philosophy for DP Installations," 2d ed., March 1977, pp. 17–22.

Therefore, we shall now review each of these key plans and programs to gain insight as to their typical composition, nature, and requirements. This review may provide either a start for your data security program or a measure of comparison and assessment for your currently existing organizational plans and programs.

VITAL RECORDS PLAN

In Chapter 2 we discussed the vital records plan as a critical element of system security. Its prime purpose is to protect data and programs that are essential to ensure proper business operation and function. They may be totally unrelated to data processing, such as blueprints, drawings, and licenses, or they may be specifically a part of data processing, such as tapes, disks, printouts, manuals, and the like.

Vital records are the business records that an organization requires in order to:

- Ensure capability to meet commitments to customers and creditors.
- Prevent the loss of large amounts of money.
- Maintain proof of stockholder interests.
- Safeguard employees' rights and equities.
- Carry out the effective and efficient reconstruction of its business following a disaster.

The *vital records plan* should present the most efficient and economical methods for protecting these records and for making them readily available for both emergency operations and disaster recovery.

Before vital records can be protected, *they must be identified*. One method is to categorize all data records according to the National Fire Protection Association's four classes: vital, important, useful, and nonessential. I prefer the terms vital, essential, important, and useful, and take "vital" to mean "irreplaceable." Chapter 2 (p. 13) defines each of these categories.

WHAT IS VITAL?

Intelligent judgment is needed as to what records are indeed *vital*. The focus should be on the functions necessary for the survival of the business. Those records that are essential to *keep the business in business* are to be defined vital. Therefore, *management must be involved* in determining the organization's vital records. It is not a data processing responsibility; it is an organizational responsibility!

The steps and strategies in a vital records plan may be summarized as follows:

1. Identify those records which are vital to the organization's continued operation.
2. Establish means to protect them.
   (a) Provide for conditioned, secure off-site storage.
   (b) Provide for adequately protected storage on-site.
3. Keep them current.
   (a) Develop update cycles for on-site records.
   (b) Develop update cycles for off-site records.
4. Establish means to reconstruct records within a reasonable time if disaster should strike.
   (a) Access control plan.
   (b) Emergency response plan.
   (c) Interim processing plan.
   (d) Restoration plan.

Step 4 emphasizes a notable point. That is, all the basic management plans and programs for data security interleave one another. *Each plan depends on and/or contributes to another.* Obviously, there is no single best plan. Rather there are a series of preplanned processes for achieving the final objective: continuance of business operation on a near-normal basis.

ACCESS CONTROL PLAN

The *access control plan* pertains to general access to the business premises. Its purpose is to limit access to a location to only those people who work there. Evidence of such plans can be seen in guards, the installation of man-traps, and the coded badge, key, and card systems used in many organizations for security.

A necessary provision in this plan (which is generally missing) is the controlled access of personnel during and immediately following a disaster. For example, if a fire should destroy part of your facility, what immediate controls do you have to control the spectators and others who march through the rubble? Who knows whom? Who vouches for whom?

Once a fire is extinguished, the fire department leaves! Management cannot rely upon intermittent police surveillance for adequate control of the remains. Furthermore, should any of the remains be moved or even tampered with, the insurance on that particular resource may be voided.

Several strategies may be used to strengthen general access control, as described below.

Localizing of Control

Delegate responsibility, authority, and control to as low a level as possible, so that each local area provides access control in addition to the customary grounds control of fences, guards, and patrols. Adequate training and drills are necessary to ensure proper responsiveness from all delegates.

Use of Multiple Control Points

Access within an area needs to be controlled. Therefore, using multiple control points in a concentric or ringlike arrangement enhances the security of the entire facility. The concept of protective rings of control is used for physical access as well as electronic access to organizational resources.

Adaptation of Control Strategy to Population Size

The size of an organization definitely influences the control strategy employed. In small companies everyone knows everyone. This is hardly true in large organizations. Therefore, additional controls of varying nature must be used as the size or populace of the organization increases.

The most secure strategy allows no one entry! As entrances and exits are provided, security is compromised. Common sense points to having as few entries and egresses as possible. Sensitive areas within an organization (DP center, mailroom, corporate management) should have additional control barriers for admittance.

The use of keys, locks, badges, and cards may be all that is required for adequate protection in small populations. However, as the organization grows, TV cameras, patrols, and computer-activated controls are necessary. Some areas may require an escort service to assure limitation to and from a defined location. This prevents inadvertent wandering or exploring by either employees or guests.

Noting of Variances; Follow-up

Surveillance with responsive action to any abnormality increases the effectiveness of an access control program. Once again, security is everyone's responsibility. Employees should challenge any stranger entering or leaving their area. All emloyees should be encouraged to report to Security *any* unusual or abnormal occurrence.

An awareness program can strengthen this facet of access control. It may be implemented by videotapes, circulated in-house memos, meetings, or other effective methods for communications in your organization. Many employees have no feeling as to just what is "normal." For example, abnormal may be:

- Employees without badges
- Visitors without escorts
- Use of emergency-only doors
- Entry after hours
- Absence of guard
- Family visitation and tour
- Tailgating

Testing the Access-Control Plan

All plans need to be tested in order to assess effectiveness. Authorized attempts should be made periodically by selected strangers to gain access to restricted areas. The success and failure of all such planned attempts should be documented and later reviewed for possible corrective action.

A substitute guard may be assigned to:

- Allow an entry without ID (Will the employees report?)
- Attempt entry into restricted areas
- Be absent from his post
- Not file any due reports

Such tests should always be carefully controlled. Managment notification and approval must be granted before *toying* with the current access system.

EMERGENCY RESPONSE PLAN

An *emergency response plan* permits immediate response to serious as well as noncatastrophic threats. Its purpose is to limit critical resource damage as well as preserve the business capability. It is not a recovery plan but rather an action plan to mitigate, if not avoid, loss of business essentials at the moment of occurrence. Threats from acts of God or acts of humans (fire, flood, explosion, riot, and so on) should be met with planned actions to preserve both the people and the business. Other related plans will assist in backup and restoration.

Several strategies may be used to initially limit damage to critical resources and protect business capability:

- Protect resources in order of human and business importance rather than their difficulty to be replaced or recovered (Data may have more business importance than people if anyone having the data can run the business.)
- Communicate an alarm to all parties affected
- Evacuate and shelter people
- Protect essential equipment
- Test the emergency response plan
- Drills—regular though nonscheduled

INTERIM PROCESSING PLAN

Once the initial emergency has taken place, a plan needs to be available to handle the time period between loss of business capability and restoration. Such a plan, activated by the emergency response plan, is called the *interim processing plan*; it consists of a description of what *both* Data Processing and the business do to keep the business going after a disaster occurs until the normal DP capability is restored. This plan defines the expected and tested approaches selected for business continuity. These approaches are for user alternate procedures as well as DP contemporary processing alternatives.

The interim processing plan provides for continuance of business capability via any means until restoration takes place. Its key strategies are:

- Definition of the user's responsibilities
- Organizational level-by-level alternate plans

- Individual action plans
- Identification of critical applications
- Identification of critical configurations
- Identification of DP temporary processing alternatives
- Assignment of interim processing duties and responsibilities (teams, tasks)
- Provision for adequate security in an interim processing situation
- Testing of the interim processing plan

An effective interim processing plan is one that has previously completed all the key strategies before called upon for use. That is, the plans *must* be in place before the accident occurs! This also prevents conflict in assignment of personnel to emergency, interim, and recovery plan activity. Employees may be assigned to more than one plan as long as there is no conflict and a secondary individual backup has been identified.

The interim processing plan necessitates outside contact and support that is committed and bound by legal agreement. Words of assurance are valueless. However, legal contracts generate two major dangers. First, the more that is stated, the more restrictions are imposed on the capability for flexibility and alternative action. Second, a false sense of adequate security may be based on a committed document. Even a signed contract does not guarantee that such support will be granted at the time you need it. For example, if the owner of the support needs it also at that moment, he may simply tell you to "sue me." The only effective interim processing plan is a tested, workable, proven plan that is retested periodically with trained people.

RESTORATION PLAN

The *restoration plan* is the third major link in the chain of disaster recovery and related asset-protection plans. Its purpose is to recover the primary data processing capability once lost. This plan is the responsibility of the provider of DP service. The scope of the restoration project is a function of the nature and extent of the damage experienced. The restoration plan complements the emergency and interim processing plans and, like them, must exist in all functions and at all levels.

The restoration plan anticipates the worst condition that might occur or be expected. Strategies must be in place to manage people, space, equipment, communications, data, and supplies in such an event. Activities that may be an integral part of this plan are:

- Determining if the old site is usable
- Making definite personnel assignments
- Providing for personnel replacement and reassignment
- Establishing communications between management and all personnel
- Identifying alternate sites
- Identifying sources of replacement equipment, including communications facilities
- Providing for the availability of data and supplies
- Creating multiple copies of the restoration plan
- Distributing copies of the restoration plan to secure remote sites
- Walkthrough of the restoration plan

DATA CLASSIFICATION PROGRAM

The *data classification program* differs from the vital records plan. Vital records were classified according to urgency and immediate need to maintain the business. Data classification is viewed in terms of sensitivity and cost. It focuses more on disclosing information that is constantly available. The classification names assigned are generally indications of the level of protection needed; for example, the familiar scheme used in the military assigns labels of Top Secret, Secret, Confidential, and Restricted.

The purpose of a data classification program is to label all media with a name best representing the level of protective measures appropriate to the data recorded on them. "Top Secret" as used by the military implies highly sensitive, highly controlled data. Rules, regulations, standards, and procedures are precisely defined for anyone coming in contact with a document thus marked. Many variables determine the who, what, where, when, why, how, and how long for use of the data.

A primary decision factor in classifying data is the consequences to the business of disclosure, modification, or destruction of the data. This determines not only sensitivity but also cost. The most appropriate cost to associate with the data may be any of the following:

- Cost of replacement
- Cost of correction
- Cost of recovering property associated with the data
- Cost of replacing property associated with the data
- Cost of recovering property controlled by the data
- Cost of replacing data controlled by the data
- Cost of lost revenue associated with data service
- Cost of lost competitive advantage
- Cost of lost business opportunity
- Cost of compensation for personal damage (being sued)

Although it is management's responsibility to set forth the rules for data classification, the *owners* of the data perform the actual classification. They alone have the necessary knowledge for affixing the most appropriate label. The strategies to be employed in a data classification program are:

- Complete labeling (Top Secret, Secret, Confidential, Restricted, Proprietary, Not To Be Reproduced, Internal Use Only, Authorized Personnel Only, Management Authorization Required, and so on)
- Precise definitions of each label
- Discipline of violators
- Relating to awareness program

The danger in any data classification scheme is *over*classification. Does one word make the entire file "Top Secret"? It is generally best to keep the number of different classifications to a minimum. Furthermore, all classifications should have termination dates for reassessment. Rule of thumb: "Classify only what really needs classification, and then, limit the classified amount." Overcontrolled data is unavailable data to those who need it to meet their business objectives.

RISK ASSESSMENT PROGRAM

This program should not be confused with a risk analysis study as proposed in Chapter 9. The purpose of a *risk assessment program* is to help management understand and fulfill its DP asset protection responsibilities. It is *not* to quantify exposures in economic ($cost/loss) terms for selecting control alternatives.

A risk assessment program requires management to evaluate its asset protection posture against a corporate guideline such as presented in Appendix B. An effective tool for doing this is a self-assessment risk questionnaire as presented in Appendices A and F.

Use of Appendix A

The Security Assessment Questionnaire presented in Appendix A is distributed to management, particularly DP management, to assist them in making a self-assessment of their security position. It affords the opportunity to conduct a private self-audit of one's security posture. The results highlight those areas needing closer attention and resolution for effective control.

The assessment is simple. It focuses on three key security areas and fourteen related categories:

I. Physical Security
   1. Fire (Questions 1–13)
   2. Rising water (Questions 14–16)
   3. Falling water (Questions 17–22)
   4. Intrusion (Questions 23–29)

II. Controls and Procedures
   5. Organizational controls (Questions 1–9)
   6. Personnel (Questions 10–14)
   7. Operational controls (Questions 15–20)
   8. Interface controls (Questions 21–26)
   9. Application development (Questions 27–33)
  10. Other (Questions 34–38)

III. Contingency Planning
  11. General (Questions 1–8)
  12. Emergency (Questions 9–13)
  13. Backup (Questions 14–19)
  14. Recovery (Questions 20–21)

Most managers rate very well in category I, Physical Security. It is categories II and III where most improvement can be made, particularly interface controls and application development. These areas often enter the "D" category: high risk, action indicated!

The categories of "A" (majority Yes answers) to "D" (majority No answers) permit a quick summarization of the manager's security position. The manager may now decide what action he will take, if any.

Use of Appendix F

Appendix F is a more elaborate presentation of risk assessment viewed from a different perspective. For instance, the section on "Purpose" emphasizes fulfillment of asset protection responsibilities in accordance with specific corporate policy. It relates the assessment to the stated corporate policy guidelines presented in Appendix B. This aids the assessor in understanding both the intent and relevance of the question before making a response.

The effective use of IBM's DP Asset Protection Self-Assessment Guide is presented in the section in Appendix F entitled "How to Use This Guide." Anyone interested in understanding its implementation should first note the four key sections:

- General Assessment
- Owner Assessment
- Custodian Assessment
- User Assessment

Note also that this document is tied to the Corporate Instruction Policy Guide for clarification and understanding of management's statement of position with regard to that particular issue. For example, Appendix F, question 3, "Are all of your developed application programs classified at least internal use only?", refers to D3 in Appendix B. A summary is provided and attachments are included to document security exposures identified and committed (Attachment A) or not committed for resolution (Attachment B).

Each level of management must assess the risk to which it may be exposed. The use of the self-assessment questionnaire provides each manager the necessary tool to personally review his or her security status. A manager has three possible responses to each item on the questionnaire:

1. In Compliance
2. Not in Compliance (for which the manager must then provide a compliance plan describing *when* and *how* he or she will come into compliance)

3. Risk Acceptance (no viable alternatives exist; a business case is made to accept the risk)

Response 3 requires a risk analysis. The rigors of an in-depth risk analysis are generally not needed. The call for such a study, however, must be examined carefully to ensure that the study doesn't cost more than the defined risk. Many measures that dramatically improve security are very inexpensive and quite effective. One should strive to use no more resources than necessary to get the job done.

SUMMARY

In closing, we remark that the data security plans, programs, policies, and guidelines just outlined are directed primarily at the data asset. However, they apply to *all* resources, and, when viewed as such, constitute a total asset protection plan and program.

Of highest importance is the evidence that proves to management these plans *do* work. Although all these plans are well documented and collectively constitute an excellent reference, THE END PRODUCT IS NOT A PAPER PRODUCT! The end product must be a provable capability—accomplished only through testing, testing, and more testing.

PART 2: ROLE OF THE SECURITY ADMINISTRATOR

BASIC ROLE

The security administrator is responsible for the physical and logical security of operational, procedural, and descriptive data and all other information systems resources using data. Obviously, no one person can perform such a task alone. Security must be treated as both a line and staff function across the organization. It is institutionalized in that it permeates the entire organization on a level-by-level basis.

Each level of management is responsible for all owners, custodians, and users of data assigned to it. Managers have an umbrella-type responsibility to the organization with respect to data security. That is, they have personal responsibility for the knowledge, awareness, authoritative assignment, education, control, plans, and programs for use or misuse of the data assets under their jurisdiction. They are expected to meet this obligation through judicious assignment and delegation of responsibility to others under their control. Much like a captain of a ship, each manager is responsible for activities under his or her command.

The basic role of the security administrator is service to management to make proper security easy. Care should be taken not to assign to the administrator responsibilities that properly belong to line management.

The security administrator does just as the title implies. He or she *administers* the data security program. This necessitates direct contact and awareness of activity with:

- *Suppliers of service.* Network manager, operations manager, data center manager, data administration manager, systems programming manager, applications development manager, and change control manager
- *Users/owners.* User/owner managers and/or assigned representatives from all pertinent business functions, operations, systems programming, applications development, and change control
- *Management.* All levels, staff, and, in particular, disaster recovery and organizational security
- *Outsiders.* Consultants, legislative/regulatory agencies, security products vendors, insurance companies, and data security organizations
- *Audit.* Internal audit, EDP audit, audit committee, and external audit
- *Legal.* Internal council, external consultant

DUTIES AND RESPONSIBILITIES

A more specific list of duties and responsibilities can be developed for the data security administrator as follows:

1. Provide direct administrative support for installed security systems to ensure the secure use of all on-line and information systems.
2. Set objectives for future development of security systems for evolving on-line and information systems.
3. Determine special resource requirements such as manpower, training, and equipment and develop plans, schedules, and cost data relative to various security responsibilities.

4. Negotiate with multiple levels of programming support management to assure integration of assigned security objectives with the long-range data processing strategy.
5. Continually review and evaluate security alternatives to determine course of action based upon technical implications, knowledge of business objectives, and corporate asset protection policy, procedures, and requirements.
6. Assure that assigned projects meet corporate security objectives and are completed according to schedule within committed costs; inform management as early as possible of problems that could materially affect objectives, schedules, and costs; recommend alternative solutions.
7. Monitor the use of all on-line and information systems to detect and act upon unauthorized access and use of proprietary business data.
8. Interface and coordinate with legal, insurance, and security staff handling internal security investigations on a highly confidential basis.
9. Conduct security audits, participate in security evaluations, and provide guidance and assistance, as requested, to facilitate the implementation of data processing asset protection programs.
10. Supervise documentation efforts associated with various internal security systems.

CAPABILITIES

A data security administrator is a specially talented individual. This person must be capable of:

- Recognizing actual and potential security exposures.
- Developing solutions in a constantly changing environment of computer technology (i.e., virtual systems, realtime, DB/DC).
- Correlating highly specialized confidential data to realtime as well as batch security systems.
- Setting security design standards for application programs.
- Establishing administrative procedures and programming development criteria for future security systems.

PR: Primary responsibility
MA: Must approve
MC: Must be consulted
MN: Must be notified
YC: May be consulted

FUNCTIONS	Data security administrator	Owner	Top management	Auditor	Custodian	D p management	Legal dept.	Data base administrator	User	Others	(Training) Standards comm.	(Production) Systems programmer	(Copy manager) (Disaster recovery) Administrator
Identify sensitive data resources	MC	PR	MA	MC	MC	MC	MC	MA	MA				
Identify risks that may impact the data resources	PR	MC	MA	MC	MN	MN	YC	YC	MN MA				
Quantify the value of impaired data	MC	PR	YC	MC	MN	YC	MC	MC	—				
Identify potential protective measures	PR	—	—	YC	—	YC	—	—	—				
Evaluate effectiveness of protective measures	PR	MC	MN	YC	—	MC	—	—	—				
Recommend protective measures	MC	PR	MA	MC	YC	MA	MA	MC	MC				
Determine resource requirements to implement protective measures	PR	MC	MA	YC	YN	MA	MA	MA	—				
Obtain management commitment to implement protective measures	PR	YN	MC	MC	MC	MC	MC	MC	—				
Control implementation of protective measures	MA	MA	YC	MC	MA	YC	MA	MA	—				
Develop and enforce security standards	PR	MC	PR	YC	MN	MN	MC	MN	—				
Conduct security audits for operational systems, systems in development	PR	—	MA	MN	—	MN YC	YC	YC	—				
Monitor for security variances during operation	PR	MN	YN	YN	YN	YN	YN	YN	—				
Coordinate data usage among functional departments	MN	MA	YC	MC	MC	YC	YC	PR	—				
Recommend and administer management's plans, programs	PR	MC	MA	MC	—	MC	MC	MC	—				
Responsibility for security education and awareness	PR	—	—	—	—	—	—	—	—				

Figure 4.1

48

- Negotiating and influencing middle and senior management on risk analysis issues concerning security versus utility of computer resources.

Such a position demands highly innovative action with little dependence on past experiences. Working with currently available, state-of-the-art tools affords the data security administrator minimal guidance in developing unique solutions to existing and future security exposures. The administrator must have the self-confidence and initiative necessary to perform his or her function using only broad management guidelines in determing both day-to-day and long-range goals.

FUNCTIONAL MATRIX

There is no fully accepted (set) job description for a data security administrator. This job has multitudinous functions, depending on many organizational variables (its nature, interface with technology, location, size, industrial position, and so on). Nevertheless, it is possible for each organization to determine who should be doing what, and what the specific responsibility of the data security administrator is, by using a functional matrix.

Figure 4.1 presents an example of a functional matrix used for defining who:

PR: has primary responsibility
MA: must approve
MC: must be consulted
MN: must be notified
YC: may be consulted

in performance of the stated function.

The horizontal elements represent people in your organization who may be involved with the functions to be performed. The vertical elements are the various functions you have defined to be performed in the data security environment. The development of the matrix depends solely on *your* organization's view of who does what. The matrix is just a tool to aid in that finding and/or definition. If nothing else, simplify the process by considering only primary responsibility. At least that classifies whose job each function is.

The data security administrator may decide to work up a functional assignment matrix alone and then present it to management for review, discussion, and finalization. Or a representative group of people affected by the assignments may develop the matrix collectively and then submit the completed document to management for approval. There is no one best way to do it. The key issue is getting it done!

Once again, such a procedure aids in affixing accountability. Although the data security administrator has general responsibility for all data security, the appropriate person or persons should be directly accountable for specific functional actions. The functional matrix helps identify these people, resolve conflicts, build awareness, and establish the overall role of the data security administrator.

As time passes, it may be advantageous to repeat this exercise or one of a similar nature. The data security administrator's role definitely involves a moving target. New functions, new business directions, and new organizational structures will constantly evolve. The job is performed in an ever-changing environment.

5

IDENTIFYING EXPOSURES

DEFINITION

The dictionary defines *exposure* as the act or instance of revealing, laying open, or subjecting to any action or influence. This definition, when used with respect to DP system security, can be misleading and cause much confusion. For example, in system design such possible acts are viewed as threats. Hence, the terms exposure and threat may be used interchangeably.

From a purist point of view, a *threat* (hazard) is an expression of intent (or the potential) to inflict harm, such as burning a building or smoking in a flammable area. The consequence or result of that action—namely, the destruction of the building—is the actual exposure. The exposure may then be quantified and expressed in monetary terms through risk analysis as a $500,000 loss. A clear distinction, therefore, does exist between threat and exposure, and we shall use that distinction. DATA EXPOSURE IS THE RESULT OR CONSEQUENCE TO DATA OF ADVERSE ACTIONS OR EVENTS.

APPROACH

A straightforward approach to identifying exposures is to sit down and list all the undesirable things that can possibly happen to data. This approach, however, is not very practical. An almost endless list of bad things can happen to data. The resources (people, time, money) required to perform the study, therefore, are tremendous, and the results often are questionable. For example, at the conclusion of such a study, what certainty exists that all the possible bad things are on our list? Furthermore, are the ones identified the most critical?

A better approach narrows the scope by concentrating on the basic *effects*[1] resulting from adverse actions or events rather than the threats or hazards to data. The use of the definition of data security affords this opportunity. As stated earlier, data security is the protection of data from unauthorized *disclosure, modification* and/or *destruction* whether accidental or intentional. Disclosure, modification, and destruction are exposures (the results or consequences to data of adverse actions or events). Data security, therefore, is simply the protection of data from six basic exposures: accidental disclosure, accidental modification, accidental destruction, intentional disclosure, intentional modification, and intentional destruction. The denial of processing capability is regarded as a separate issue. However, to simplify the identification process and analysis, the delay or loss of availability data may also be grouped into these six basic exposures under the category of accidental/intentional data destruction. A system's being down for 30, 60, or more minutes means that the data is unavailable (i.e., assumed destroyed) during that period. Plans will have to be made for effective interim action and control. Therefore, all the undesirable things that can happen to data may be grouped into the following six basic exposures:

1. *Accidental disclosure*—the unintentional revealing of data. Examples of accidental disclosure are:
   - Output delivered to the wrong user
   - Transmission to the wrong terminal
   - Passwords taped on the side of terminals
   - Trash copies of printouts used for personal scrap
   - Data displayed but unattended
2. *Accidental modification*—the unintentional change of data. Examples of accidental modification are:
   - Transposition error
   - Hardware malfunction
   - Software malfunction
   - Duplication

---

[1]Robert H. Courtney, Jr., "Security Risk Assessment in Electronic Data Systems," IBM Publication TR21.700-A, revised March 1981, p. 9.

3. *Accidental destruction*—the unintentional absence of data. Examples of accidental destruction are:
   - Acts of God: fire, tornado, flood, and so on.
   - Unknowingly writing over a "good" file
   - Dropping a disk pack
   - Losing a message
   - Indefinite wait period
4. *Intentional disclosure*—the deliberate act of revealing data. Examples of intentional disclosure are:
   - Personal retention and perusal of printout carbons
   - Selling information
   - Breaking into a data file
   - Dumping sensitive data
   - Distributing data to unauthorized people
5. *Intentional modification*—the deliberate act of changing data. Examples of intentional modification are:
   - Rewriting a file
   - Adding data
   - Deleting data
   - Substitution
   - Withholding data
6. *Intentional destruction*—the deliberate act of removing data. Examples of intentional destruction are:
   - Riots
   - Sabotage
   - Hiding
   - Stealing
   - Use of destructive devices: magnet, degausser, explosives, and so on

AREAS OF CONCERN

The effort necessary to perform an adequate job in identifying exposures can be reduced further by knowing where to look. Chapter 2 discussed key areas of concern in past information systems. Several practitioners in the field of data security have developed their list of areas of concern. For example:

1. Jerry FitzGerald [2] lists the following:

[2]Jerry FitzGerald, "EDP Risk Analysis for Contingency Planning," *EDPACS,* VI: 2 (August 1978, 6–8.

- Fraud or defalcation
- Privacy
- Information control policies
- Errors and omissions
- Message loss or change
- Disasters and disruptions
- Information security/theft
- Recovery and restart
- Backup facilities
- Unauthorized program changes
- Documentation
- Computer program-generated transactions
- Record retention and destruction
- Negotiable documents control
- Illegal penetration
- Access control
- Audit trails
- Program/data validation
- Management control and reporting
- Segregation of duties
- Reliability
- Transaction entry error handling
- Hardware errors
- Output balancing reconciliation

2. James Martin[3] presents this list:
   - Acts of God
   - Hardware and program failures
   - Human carelessness
   - Malicious damage
   - Crime
   - Invasion of privacy

3. Mair, Wood, and Davis[4] listed the following for an information processing facility:
   - Human errors
   - Hardware/software failures
   - Computer abuse
   - Catastrophe

4. John Busch, Jr., and Joseph Sardinas, Jr.,[5] present the following list of hazards:
   - Malfunctions
   - Fraud and unauthorized access
   - Power and communications failures
   - Fires
   - Sabotage and riot

---

[3]James Martin, *Security, Accuracy and Privacy in Computer Systems*, (Englewood Cliffs, N.J.: Prentice-Hall, Inc., 1973), pp. 12–13.

[4]W. C. Mair, W. R. Wood, and K. W. Davis, *Computer Control & Audit*, 11A (1978), 363.

[5]J. C. Busch, Jr., and J. L. Sardinas, Jr., *Computer Control & Audit: A Total Systems Approach* (New York: John Wiley & Sons, 1978), pp. 215–216.

- Natural disasters
- General hazards

5. Robert H. Courtney, Jr.,[6] lists the following generic threats:
   - Fire
   - Water
   - Communications failures
   - Power failures
   - Data entry errors
   - Programming errors

The idea behind classifying concerns into areas is the same as that behind classifying exposures into six basic consequences—that is, to simplify the process of identification. There are no perfect classifications. However, these classifications are a definite aid to the systems designer and auditor. They help to get the job *done* as efficiently and effectively as possible.

CAUSAL AGENTS

A small list of general causal agents seems most appropriate in simplifying the identification process. A summary of the abovementioned lists might be: People, Hardware, Software, Communications, Acts of God, and Procedure (absence or insufficiency of).

The system designer and auditor can now develop basic questions regarding data security using the list of exposures and causal agents. For example:

How can . . .

People			disclose data?
Hardware	accidentally		
Software			modify data?
Communications	intentionally		
Acts of God			
Procedure			destroy data?

Such a list still produces an enormous number of possible questions. In order to develop a list of effective questions, the area of identification must be significantly reduced. That is to say, the investigation of exposures must be done within predefined boundaries. The study of the system must be broken into meaningful pieces or *chunks*. For example, rather than ask, "How can people accidentally disclose data in this sys-

[6]Robert H. Courtney, Jr., "Security Risk Assessment in Electronic Data Processing Systems," IBM Publication TR21.700-A, revised March 1981, p. 14.

tem?'', we focus the question on a specific area: "How can people accidentally disclose this file at the time of recording?"

The key, then, is to develop a meaningful framework within which systems can be *chunked* effectively. The use of a data control life cycle as presented in Chapter 6 provides this tool. Questioning can now be confined to identifying exposures at specific control points. This process will be used as a basis for the methodology described in Chapters 6 through 12.

Since the identification process may be one of individual preference, the author advocates the use of *any* technique that helps provide acceptable (adequate, credible) results in minimum time. The practitioner may decide to use any one or combination of existing techniques—that is, focusing on the critical control areas (Chapter 2), literature search, interviews, brainstorming, threat scenarios, self-assessment questionnaires (Appendices A and F), system walkthroughs, audit reviews, grid analysis, risk consultant services, or other suggested approaches such as the data exposure life cycle presented in Chapter 6. The correct technique is the one that is most appropriate to use in your organization at the time requested.

6

EXPOSURE CONTROL POINTS

An effective, proven approach to designing data processing systems is the use of a tool known as the *system development life cycle* or *project life cycle*. This tool permits the user to lay out a complex system into many small, definable process pieces. Each piece or phase of the total process, therefore, can be managed and controlled.

The auditor and system designer also need such a tool for defining and controlling information in a system. In particular, what is called for is a *data control life cycle*—a representative data flow structure across which all information travels from its inception to its demise. Such a structure would have definable chunks (phases, pieces, or points) for purposes of data control design and review.

In May of 1972, IBM participated in a multimillion-dollar data security study known as Project "SAFE."[1] This study hinted at a workable methodology for controlling data in a system. It defined eleven basic information processing steps that encompass all systems. These steps are now redefined and carried forward into a complete methodology for securing and controlling data in information systems. Collectively, they constitute a complete data control life cycle. The steps are (by design) very general in nature in order to include any system, application, and environment in which data may be processed, each step may be discretely defined to any depth deemed necessary.

---

[1]*IBM "Secure Automated Facilities Environment" Study*, Vol. 3, Part 2 (May 1972), "Study Results, State of Illinois," pp. 106, 107.

The eleven basic data exposure control points (CPs) of the data control life cycle are defined as follows:

CP1: Data Gathering.   The manual creating and transportation of data.

This is the point of inception of data into the information system. It includes any method or means by which the data originates and is collected. Typical application examples are:

- Order Entry (receipt of orders). Input and collection by telephone, messenger, salesman, walk-ins, mail, and any other means of gathering the original data input to an order.
- Payroll (receipt of obligations). Input and receipt of pay obligations to employees by timecards, timesheets, job cards, or any other form of initial debt obligation.
- Inventory (issues and receipts). Input and collection by any form or manner in which inventory is disbursed or received, such as standard forms, telephone, or personal request.

CP2: Data Input Movement.   The manual movement of source documents (at CP1) to the input area in which source documents are converted to machine-readable form.

This control point is primarily for batch-type systems. It provides a pathway for tracing the manual handling of information from its source to an area where it is transformed into machine-readable form. Typical application examples are:

- Order Entry (manual order movement). Transport by car, plane, clerk, or other entity of the initial order to a data conversion area. This includes the mailing of original documents to a data center input station.
- Payroll (movement of pay obligations). Same procedure as for Order Entry.
- Inventory (movement of issues, receipts). Same procedure as for Order Entry.

Note: Since the process at each control point is identical for all applications, only Order Entry will be illustrated as example for the remaining control points.

CP3: Data Conversion.   The physical conversion of initial source documents to machine-readable form.

At this point, the original input data to a particular system is transformed from English to a form acceptable to a computerized data processing system. A typical example in an Order Entry system would be:

- Keying of orders into a DP terminal
- Mark-sense of order transformation into digital form
- Change of any initial order information inputed to the Order Entry system to a machine-readable form

CP4: Data Communication (input). The transmission of machine-readable data.

At this control point, information is sent to a data processing facility via any means. The data may be transmitted electronically or carried by person to the DP center. This could occur in an Order Entry application by:

- Manually carrying the machine-readable order input data to the DP center. This is typical in a small batch type of operation.
- Electronically transmitting the machine-acceptable order input to the DP center.
- Transporting the machine-readable order data by any acceptable means (such as mail) to the site for input into the DP system.

CP5: Data Receipt. The receipt and storage of data via communications or manual facilities.

This control provides a data check on the receipt, acknowledgement, and storage of input information readied for processing. This would be represented in an Order Entry system in a variety of ways:

- Personal delivery of machine-readable order data to DP operations
- Receipt and acknowledgment of electronically transmitted order information readied for processing
- Storage of order input information at a DP center until time of processing

CP6: Data Processing. The execution of application programs to perform intended computations and their results.

This control point is most familiar to everyone. Unfortunately, it is generally the only point considered for control in most automated data processing operations. It is quite obvious that lack of adequate control at any of the preceding five control points would compromise any degree of data integrity at this point. This particular control point covers the control of information as it is being processed by a preprogrammed set of instructions. An Order Entry application at this time might:

- Edit-check the incoming order.
- Call any utility programs or software subroutines required to execute the actions requested.
- Update all affected business files.
- Calculate results.

CP7: Data Preparation (output).   The preparation of data output media such as cards, paper, tapes, disks, diskettes, and microfilm for dissemination to the users.

This control point focuses on the output media where the results of processing were placed. The data resides here until dissemination to the user. In an Order Entry application, the data on these media could include such prepared items as:

- Hard-copy acknowledgements.
- "Spooled" tapes and disks of formatted results.
- Audit journals, logs, registers.
- Backup recovery files.
- SMF (type) reports.

CP8: Data Output Movement.   The manual movement of computer-produced output, in various media form, to the output area to await user pickup.

This point was included to cover those systems where processed data is not instantaneously delivered to the requestor or user. The information from CP7 is held in some designated location for later pickup or transmission. For example, in Order Entry this may be:

- Hand-carrying of all backup files to the DP manager's office.
- Manual delivery of audit reports to the accounting department.
- Transporting of "spooled" tapes and disks to the DP library.
- Delivery by operations personnel of any hard-copy output to a pickup area.

CP9: Data Communication (output). The direct transmission and/or delivery of output to the user.

Most data processing facilities today have the capability of on-line realtime response. This control point's major task is the control of transmitted information available at CP7. It can also be used as a control step for the delivery of any information awaiting pickup at CP8. Therefore, in an Order Entry application, this would include any of the following actions:

- Direct transmission of processed results to the user
- Personal pickup of processed data by the user
- Authorized representative pickup of data delivered to the user

CP10: Data Usage. The use of data by the recipient, including the storage or location of data while it is being used.

This control point covers the entire timeframe from actual delivery of information to the user until the user is finished with it. This is very important! The control is not only on the user's use of the data but also on the user's retention of the information. Much information generated today is in a retrievable form. Such information must be controlled whether being used at that moment or not. For example, in Order Entry this may include:

- Review of the completed, processed order acknowledgements before delivery.
- Audit of available data logs, registers, journals.
- Copying of any processed information.
- Maintaining of all backup recovery files.
- Storage of any completed order information.

CP11: Data Disposition. The disposition of data after the period of usage, including the methods and locations of storage, length of time for storage, and final disposal, as appropriate.

At this final point, control is provided for all information once it leaves the user's domain. The data may be immediately terminated by burning, shredding, demagnetizing, and the like. Or the data may live on for possible later recall. CP11 allows control over information until it is completely terminated. In Order Entry this would include:

- Transfer of order data to final disposition.

- Off-site maintenance and storage of order information.
- Utter destruction of all order data media.

It should be obvious that some systems may skip several control points. For example, an on-line system may have no manual movement of source documents (at CP2), since all data is directly inputed into the system. On the other hand, a batch system may display the need for consideration at each control point. This is perfectly acceptable! Some applications may even jump back and forth across several points.

Remember: The eleven control points are only for use to assist in identifying, tracing, and defining control needs!

7

APPLYING THE
METHODOLOGY

In order to gain a better understanding of the concept and application of the data control life cycle methodology—the approach taken, the forms used, and the results produced—a complete example will now be given using a standard payroll system.

The data control life cycle methodology is appropriate for use in systems already designed as well as those currently being designed. Therefore, the Payroll system example may be viewed either as (1) being designed as shown in Figure 7.1 and requiring auditability and control measures, or (2) being designed as shown in Figure 7.1 and currently being audited.

The use of the eleven basic data exposure control points serve as an aid to either the systems designer or the auditor. To begin, one uses an overview document (such as Figure 7.1) of the payroll workflow. Each control point is then identified on the workflow as illustrated in Figure 7.2.

One may also identify both the activity and control point location in a payroll application by referring to existing documentation, talking directly to payroll, requesting an application walkthrough by DP, or executing design scenarios. The result might be as follows:

Control Point 1. Data Gathering
Information for the payroll system is initially generated by the

Payroll Workflow

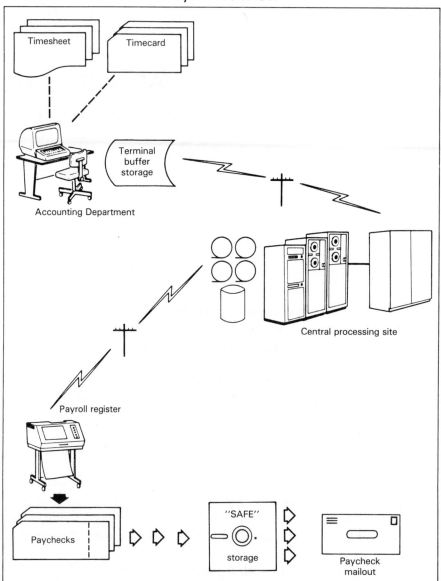

Figure 7.1

workers and recorded on either timesheets or timecards. This is the original collection of source data input to the system.

Control Point 2.   Data Input Movement
The timesheets and timecards are picked up by clerks and taken to the accounting payroll administrator for review and processing.

Payroll Workflow

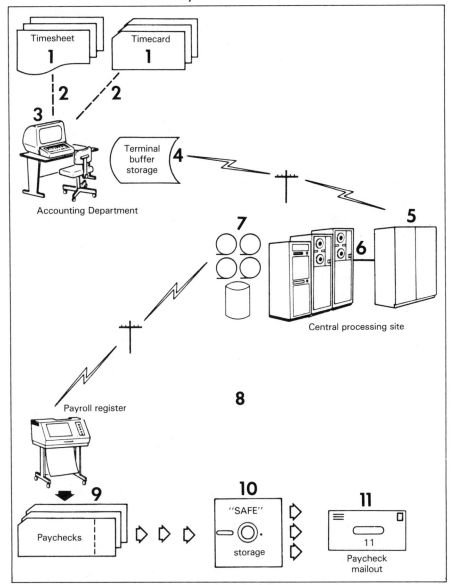

Figure 7.2

Control Point 3.   Data Conversion
The payroll administrator gives the timesheets and timecards to the
payroll data processing assistant for entry into the system. The assistant keys the original source data into a terminal that automatically converts it into machine-readable form.

Control Point 4.   Data Communication
After the payroll data has been entered into an electronic storage area (buffer) and an open transmission link established to the main data processing facility, the information is dumped out onto the line.

Control Point 5.   Data Receipt
The information sent from payroll over outside transmission lines is received at the main data processing facility. The information is dated, time-stamped, and logged for future processing.

Control Point 6.   Data Processing
The software procedures program for executing payroll is called into the system to work on the readied and waiting payroll data. The data is processed through the program and the results directed to a particular device or devices.

Control Point 7.   Data Preparation (output)
The resultant data from payroll processing is prepared on both pre-printed forms and magnetic tape.

Control Point 8.   Data Output Movement
The payroll checks and register for the local site are taken by the operator to the DP manager's office to await pickup. Here they are properly safeguarded until claimed by an authorized party.

Control Point 9.   Data Communication (output)
The prepared magnetic-tape payroll data is transmitted to various plant sites' terminal receiving stations. Users directly pick up the data or, if using CP8, go to that pickup area.

Control Point 10.   Data Usage
The payroll checks, registers, and other prepared data are reviewed by the users (payroll manager, audit, accounting, and so on). The users review, maintain, and safeguard the data until readied for disbursement to employees, prepared for off-site storage, or assigned to termination.

Control Point 11.   Data Disposition
All checks and registers are distributed. The journals and registers are safeguarded until no longer needed. Final disposition then takes place.

IDENTIFYING EXPOSURES

The payroll application has now been related to the eleven data exposure control points. The next step is to determine the specific data exposures present at each control point. Any of the techniques suggested in Chapter 5 may be used. For our purposes, a structured brainstorm session employing the concepts of basic exposures and causal agents is used for determining the data exposures of the system under design. The attendees at this session should be the people most directly associated with both the control point activity and the environment under study. This technique has proven to be effective in achieving the desired results at this stage. On the other hand, the audit and review of data exposures for a designed system has best been served by reviewing the existing documentation on exposures and controls. The absence of adequate documentation to perform this study may suggest that a quick risk analysis should be executed as set forth in Chapter 12.

In either case, a data exposure workpaper as illustrated in Figure 7.3 is of value to both the systems designer and auditor at this step. This workpaper provides a method for capturing the following information:

1. Identification of the specific control point studied
2. Identification of the specific system studied
3. Identification of the specific data exposure studied
4. A complete description of the particular data exposure studied at that control point
5. Documentation of the defined exposures

Figure 7.4 shows a completed data exposure workpaper for the payroll system at CP1. The actual number of workpapers used for any system may vary. Control points presenting a large number of data exposures for each basic exposure may necessitate several workpapers; control points having no relevance to this system would have none. Therefore, after the defining of all the exposures across the data life cycle, more or less than eleven data exposure workpapers may be completed.

The classification symbol (A1, A2, . . ., An; B1, B2, . . ., Bn, and so on) assigned to a particular exposure depends on two factors: first, the particular consequence of the basic exposure (A–F); and second, the nature of the particular exposure defined (1, 2, 3, . . .). If fraud was

Data Exposure Workpaper

Control point: **1.**		System: **2.**
Basic exposure **3.**		Complete description of data exposure
		4.
Accidental data disclosure	A	
Accidental data modification	B	
Accidental data destruction	C	
Intentional data disclosure	D	
Intentional data modification	E	
Intentional data destruction	F	

5.

Figure 7.3

first defined as a possible exposure (E1) at CP1, then at any other control point where fraud was the nature of the exposure, the classification E1 would be used again. It is conceivable that some systems may have such common exposure across all points.

Data Exposure Workpaper

Control point: ___1___		System: _PAYROLL_
Basic exposure		*Complete description of data exposure*
Accidental data disclosure	A	A1. Interruptions, such as a sudden call to the manager's office, may cause a salaried employee to leave their timesheet on their desk. Anyone dropping in could accidentally scan the sheet revealing hospital, doctor, or other personal events recorded.
Accidental data modification	B	B1. At the time the employee completes the required timecard or timesheet for hours worked on a particular job, that employee may inadvertantly transpose two or more digits of information. The type of information affected would be: hours worked, date, employee number, and job number. All of these are completed by the employee. B2. The employee cannot always recall a particular job number and, therefore, does not complete this information on the form.
Accidental data destruction	C	B3. The time mechanism in the timeclocks may malfunction. This can cause inaccurate data to be registered in the timecards as the employee clocks on/off a shift or job. B4. New accounting procedures for coding timecards. Timesheets are never explained to the employees. Notification of change is made by memo only!
Intentional data disclosure	D	C1. Cards may be lost from their racks due to heavy wind currents or misplacement. E1. An employee who is late might ask a friend to clock in for him. A friend might punch out for an employee at the end of the day, thus allowing that employee to have the afternoon off with pay.
Intentional data modification	E	F1. An employee who does not want to work on assigned job in his work cue rack may remove the card and discard it. That job, then, no longer exist.
Intentional data destruction	F	

Figure 7.4

In the payroll system example, this classification procedure is evidenced in Figure 7.5, which represents a completed workpaper for CP2. Notice that exposure C1 at CP2 (loss of timecards and timesheets) is of the same nature as exposure C1 at CP1 (loss of timecards): they *both* define the loss of timecards and timesheets. On the other hand, the basic

Data Exposure Workpaper

Control point: ____2____   System: PAYROLL

Basic exposure		Complete description of data exposure
Accidental data disclosure	A	A2. Some timesheets and timecards are not available at the time of pickup due to absence of the employee. These sheets are then turned in late and may be handled by several people until they reach the proper destination. During this process someone not normally in the transfer process may accidentally see personal information on an employee.
Accidental data modification	B	C1. The timecards and timesheets would be lost in the mail and never recovered. D1. The time records are sold to an outside party for development of mailing lists and competitive statistics.
Accidental data destruction	C	E1. The clerk who picks up and delivers the timecards, timesheets, and job cards may decide to add, change, or delete recorded data for a fee.
Intentional data disclosure	D	
Intentional data modification	E	
Intentional data destruction	F	

Figure 7.5

exposure of accidental disclosure of data at CP2 (late receipt of data) is *not* of the same nature as defined at CP1 (unattended data). Therefore, a different "A" classification is given. This classification procedure provides the capability for immediate observation of common exposures across control points. This will be discussed more fully and displayed graphically in the next step.

MAPPING EXPOSURES

The definition and classification of data exposures across the data life cycle provides all the input that is necessary to "map" a graphic picture of location and concentration. Figure 7.6 shows a matrix grid where the classification of exposures is "mapped" to their existence at each control point. Payroll has been "mapped" by way of illustration for the two control points discussed. A complete "mapping" may result in a grid as displayed in Figure 7.7. The value of "mapping" such as displayed in Figure 7.7 is the ease of identifying primary control point weakness, such as CP3, and particular exposures that are prevalent across *all* exposure points, such as C1 and E1.

The designer or auditor gains a feeling for where the resources should be applied for effective control. He or she also gains insight as to the actual site of possible exposure to a system. If no further analysis is performed or is possible at this time, "mapping" at least provides a sense of direction for the user—one step better than a guess!

Obviously, the limitation of mapping is that it does not tell us which exposures are most critical. The majority (clusters) of exposures are pictorially evident; however, the clusters may not include the exposure that most needs control. For example, exposure B1 at CP1 may occur consistently and cost the organization millions of dollars per year, yet this exposure is not highlighted—not part of the cluster.

In order to effectively apply resources to controlling the risks of data exposure, each identified exposure must be quantified. The expected dollar annual loss per year for each exposure is determined by performance of a risk analysis. Chapter 9 presents an effective technique to quantify risk and rank exposures. It may be very beneficial, however, to initially limit the potential for risk in any information system considered; Chapter 8 presents, in general, several sound security practices for doing so.

Mapping Data Exposures
to Data Control Points

Basic exposure	Data exposure control points											Type
	1	2	3	4	5	6	7	8	9	10	11	
Accidental data disclosure	A1	A2										A
Accidental data modification	B1 B2 B3 B4											B
Accidental data destruction	C1	C1										C
Intentional data disclosure		D1										D
Intentional data modification	E1	E1										E
Intentional data destruction	F1											F

Figure 7.6

Mapping Data Exposures
to Data Control Points

Basic exposure	1	2	3	4	5	6	7	8	9	10	11	Type
				Data exposure control points								
Accidental data disclosure	A1	A2	A3 A4	A3	A3	A4 A5	A3	A3	A3 A6	A3 A4	A3	A
Accidental data modification	B1 B2 B3 B4		B1 B5 B6 B7	B6	B6	B5 B6	B6		B6			B
Accidental data destruction	C1	C1	C1 C2	C1 C3	C1	C1	C1	C1	C1 C3	C1	C1	C
Intentional data disclosure		D1	D1 D2 D3 D4			D1 D2				D1 D5	D5	D
Intentional data modification	E1	E1	E1 E2 E3 E4	E1	E1	E1	E1	E1	E1	E1	E1	E
Intentional data destruction	F1		F2			F2 F3	F3					F

Figure 7.7

8

LIMITING RISK

Perhaps the key to data security lies in our capability to control or at least limit risk. How then, do we limit risk? Notice the word *limit,* not eliminate. The only totally secure system is one that is inaccessible and nonoperative. The moment any system is approachable, it entails some risk.

Listed below are some ways in which the designer can limit risk.

LIMIT DATA

In the past, data processing believed the best way to serve a user was to give him not only what was needed but also what might be of interest. The end result was an availability of information that was unwarranted and unnecessarily tempting.

Data can be effectively limited in *quantity, association, interpretation*, and *currency*. This limits the process of transforming data into meaningful information.

No bit, byte, character, or word is sensitive by itself! Everything depends on who receives the data and what he or she has available to associate with it. For example, notice the following transformation of seemingly meaningless data into information as more data becomes available for association and interpretation:

Step 1.   86152

Step 2. $861.52

Step 3. $861.52/month

Step 4. $861.52/month J. Jones

Step 5. $861.52/month J. Jones, 1970

Step 5 is interesting because it also brings out the importance of information currency. If the date had been a future one, it might imply a future projected payscale and be extremely sensitive data.

Generally, as data gets older, its sensitivity falls off. However, there are exceptions. A most notable exception was the medical records of Senator Thomas Eagleton in 1976 when nominated to run for vice-president of the United States. The disclosure of that information severely diminished the viability of his candidacy.

COUCH CONSTRAINTS WITH SERVICE

Each security measure a designer places in a system represents one more obstacle or barrier to the user of that system. At least, that is the user's mental attitude unless he or she understands the personal benefit. Any good security design, therefore, must include understandable personal benefits to the user.

The designer has an obligation to educate the user as to the benefits of all data security safeguards. If this obligation is ignored, the safeguard is ignored. For example, the design of individual password protection to a company's files is a data security safeguard. If, however, the user of the password system is not educated to the personal benefits of this protective constraint, the password will be compromised by being conveniently taped on the terminal or marked on the wall.

Most data security measures are compromised because the user consistently experiences the frustrations of the barrier but senses no personal benefit from its usage. This risk can be limited only by selling the users on what's in it for them.

In short, all designed information constraints must be couched with service in order to be accepted and practiced by users.

CONTROL DOMAINS

Risk can be limited if work areas can be controlled. These work areas, called *domains* or *spheres of influence*, must first be defined. In general, domains are defined to a particular level such as program, product, and personnel. However, a system's domain may be as discrete as a record or as global as a data processing facility. The level of domain definition depends on the level of understanding and comprehension needed to control that work area.

For example, the area where a programmer does his work is a domain; the area where a user performs his duty is a domain; and the CPU (processor) is a domain.

General domains would include: input, process, output, programming, design, test operations, users, management, and so on. Discrete domains would be possible subdivisions within each general domain. For instance, process could be presented as illustrated in Figure 8.1. Each defined area of process storage is a domain. The control concern is the activity between and among all the possible process interfaces.

To reduce risk, the designer must first define the domains in the system environment. This provides an effective means for the later consideration of appropriate controls. Such illustrations are often viewed as general security models.

CONTROL EACH INTERFACE

After the domains are identified and defined, control considerations can be focused on the activity permitted at each interface. In Figure 8.1, for example, what controls should be in place between DB Batch and the Data Access Method domains? Between Timesharing and Database Management System Services? Between User and the Communication Access Method?

Many paths through the system must be explored in order to reduce risk. Total system security may warrant the control of risk everywhere the data resource is moved outside its present domain.

ASSIGN INDIVIDUAL ACCOUNTABILITY

For every activity that occurs in the system environment, a permanent record should be available of the event that caused that action. It should be possible to trace any action performed on a resource back to the initi-

Central Processor Domains

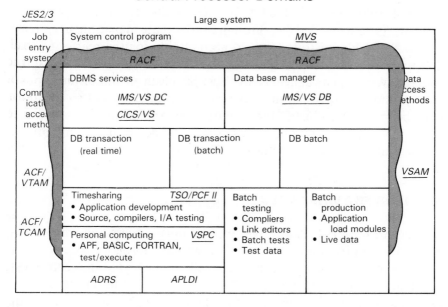

Figure 8.1

ator. In order to reduce risk, the system must have the capability of pointing back to some event causing the action and the individual responsible *and* held accountable for the action.

When a user *signs on* (establishes contact) to the system through a terminal, that user is immediately accountable for any activity performed. As data is called for, through the database management system, the database administrator is held accountable for the release of that data to the requestor. The requestor is held accountable for the use of the data received. When challenged by those people in an authoritative position (president, chief executive officer, auditor, IRS, and so on) they must be prepared to justify the activities performed.

Individual accountability acts as a strong deterrent to temptations of criminal gain and thus helps limit the data security risk.

MONITOR FOR VARIANCES

In order to limit risk in any system, one must understand what is expected for and from the system. What are the "norms" of operation?

If a construction project outside the building breaks the central water main, this action may disrupt the computer system, not necessarily by flood but rather by the lack of coolant in the coils of the CPU. An IBM System 370 Model 168, for example, must have water circulation in order to function.

A request for payroll information from the loading dock at 3 A.M. on Sunday morning may certainly be out of normal practice (norms). The security control system must monitor for such variances, whether man-made or system-made. In fact, notification of any abnormalities in business procedures should be immediately recognized, recorded, and reported.

Personnel must be trained to recognize what is normally expected from a given system. For example, a payroll clerk saw variations of ± $100/day in the receipts register. It was never reported. When later asked by an auditor why it was never reported, the clerk responded, "This has happened every day since I've been here!"

In order to limit risk, *norms* must be defined, personnel trained, and the surveillance system monitored for variances.

REPORT FOR ACTION

Once a good surveillance system is in place, the noted variances must be reported to the right people for appropriate action. It is not enough to detect an abnormality. If risk is to be limited, something *must* be done.

The action may be to do nothing or to assert some strong measure of correction—that is up to management.

For example, to limit the risk of an employee's entering an unauthorized area, a magnetic ID card system can be employed. Inserting the card into the badge reader permits entrance upon system verification of employee and work location. Any attempt to gain access to any other area using the same ID card triggers the following action:

1. Automatic logging of employee man-number, time, date, areas of authorization, and the area accessed.
2. Signaling Central Security of an unauthorized access attempt.
3. Immediate dispatch of a manager, guard, or other management surrogate to investigate attempted penetration, or a log printing of the attempt and delivery of the log to the employee's manager for final resolution. All corrective action is the province of management.

Many information systems can be designed to police themselves in critical areas. The right report to the right person at the right time reduces exposure and thereby limits risk.

9

RISK ANALYSIS

A risk analysis or risk assessment may be performed at any time. Their purposes are to:

1. Aid in the identification of exposures.
2. Assist in quantifying values for exposures.
3. Permit the ranking of exposures by priority.
4. Serve as a basis for cost-effective analysis.

Generally, a risk assessment focuses on purposes 1 and 2. A risk analysis is more comprehensive and has as its objective all 4 purposes. In short, the objective is to quantify the existing exposures so that a *basis* may be established for the later selection of appropriate cost-effective security controls (Chapters 10, 11).

GUIDE FOR CONTROL

Obviously, not all exposures need to be or should be controlled. Total control is not cost-effective and generally is very inefficient. However, if the designer has no idea which exposure presents the greatest overall risk in terms of frequency of occurrence and cost, he has no alternative but to control every exposure. The adequacy of control depends on knowing the relative cost to the business for the exposures not controlled.

A risk analysis, therefore, offers the designer and the auditor a guide for controls. This being the case, the most appropriate time for a study of this nature is *before* the consideration of controls.

IDENTIFYING EXPOSURES

A risk analysis calls for the assessment of the risks or exposures of the entity under study. The techniques to be employed may be a literature search, interviews, brainstorming, threat scenarios, self-assessment questionnaires, system walkthroughs, audit reviews, grid analysis, risk consultant services, or other suggested approaches such as the data exposure life cycle presented in Chapter 6.

The objective of the identification phase in a risk analysis is to define the existing major exposures. *Any* technique that easily provides this information with a sense of adequacy and credibility is the right one to choose. Refer to Chapter 5 for more discussion of the identification of exposures.

KEY FACTOR

The key factor in the performance of a risk analysis is the extent of exactness. The pitfall often encountered by the practitioner is that of being too precise. This often leads to the analysis becoming a career instead of a study!

The analyst must remember that the final objective of the analysis is to permit a ranking of the risk. This necessitates only a relative magnitude in cost (loss) and probability assignment. As Courtney[1] has observed: "The key is to use a technique that is sufficiently inexact, permitting the study to be adequately performed in reasonable time."

A *danger* often encountered in studies of this nature is that more is spent to provide management with information on which to base a decision than is at risk. One must ward off irrational behavior where the risk assessment is more expensive than the acceptance of the risk. The study need only be as exact as is necessary for the decision that will be made from it.

A simple risk assessment program as outlined in Chapter 4, or a "quik" approach as outlined in Chapter 12, may be all that is initially

[1]"Security Risk Assessment in Electronic Data Processing Systems," IBM Publication TR21.700-A, Systems Communications Division, Kingston, N.Y. 12401, revised March 1981, 35 pp.

called for. A detailed analysis should still take no more than three to six weeks to perform. An aid to achieving this goal is to use the following:

1. A risk analysis team
2. Ballpark values
3. Subjective cost (loss) and probability range tables

THE APPROACH

The method originally proposed by Robert H. Courtney, Jr., and published by the National Bureau of Standards[2] uses all three properties listed above. James Martin presented this approach in his book entitled, *Security, Accuracy and Privacy in Computer Systems*, and Dr. Jerry FitzGerald published the same approach with a modification in the table matrices in the *EDPAudit, Control and Security Newsletter (EDPACS)*, Vol. 9, No. 5. As of today, this is the only approach endorsed by the federal government, and it is now presented for your consideration.

RISK ANALYSIS TEAM

A risk analysis study generally cuts across multiple functional areas, requiring more time than one person can give to finish it before it becomes obsolete. Therefore, a team of people is usually selected. The selection of such a team depends on the depth of knowledge and experience each member brings to the total area under study. This team should have a management sponsor. The typical sponsor is the application owner executive of the system under study.

Usually the participants in a risk team are senior in experience, knowledge, and/or position for the study area. They most often are comprised of:

- DP operations management
- User management
- Application programmers
- Systems programmers

[2]"Guideline for Automatic Data Processing Risk Analysis," National Bureau of Standards, Federal Information Processing Standards Publication (FIPS) 65, August 1, 1979, 27 pp.

- Internal audit
- Security administrator
- Quality control
- Database administrator (if available)

The security administrator is most often selected as the team leader. He represents the chief executive officer because of his close tie to top management and, when chosen, he is the leader and coordinator but not a representative of an area under study. Some additional considerations pertaining to the team candidates are:

- Appointed by senior management.
- Well-informed, competent people.
- Senior in experience and/or position.
- Full-time or half-time assignment.
- *Never* part-time assignment.
- Work in a project mode (objectives, goals, checkpoints, deliverables, and so on).

CRITICAL SUCCESS FACTOR

A data security study must have full management support. Top management must *commit* the resources necessary to perform this study. Their consent but not commitment on such a project has been the primary reason for so-called failure in studies of this nature. A study that has received only management's consent leads only to busy work, false expectations, and frustration. A full management policy must be formulated and stated, as elaborated on in Chapter 4.

This need for commitment is mentioned at this point only to insure that the risk team has the management support necessary to gather the data required. Otherwise, the team will experience the great *put-off* or complete unavailability of data owners/users. Result: from an acceptance and credibility view, the better choice is to disband and spend your time more profitably elsewhere.

If a study is important enough to do, it is important enough to do right—and that begins with management's full support and commitment.

ELEMENTS OF RISK (R)

Basically, there are two major elements to risk: P, the probability of an exposure's occurring a given number of times per year, and C, the cost or loss attributed to such an exposure. The relationship between these two elements may be simply expressed as

$$R = P \times C$$

The risk is generally expressed in terms of loss dollars per year, where probability is defined in terms of expected rate of occurrence.

PROBABILITY VALUE (P)

Each defined exposure for a given resource has a likelihood of occurrence, called the *probable exposure*, or the probability of a specific exposure occurring. It is expressed as a probability value, P. The probability value, P, is best obtained from the owners and users of the resource. These people are generally most familiar with the resource and its associated exposures.

The actual value assigned to P is best expressed in terms other than finite percentages, such as 87.5%. Such values are very difficult to elicit from a particular owner or user. Furthermore, such exactness is absurd and is not necessary for quantifying the probability of a particular occurrence. A better approach is to state the probabilities in terms to which the owner or user can most easily relate. These terms are ranges of time, generally expressed as expected rates of occurrence. For example, the question is asked, "Would you say that the frequency of accidentally destroying the Accounts Payable file is once in three years, once a year, once a month, or once a day?" An actual range of values is used for the owner's and user's selection. This greatly eases the pressure of giving a definitive response.

Table 9.1 illustrates a typical range table used in the assigning of probability values for defined exposures. If an estimate lies wthin a range, say twice a year, then the closest time value to that estimate is used. In this case that would be once in 100 days. The subjective probability values (i.e., once in 300 years, and so on) are converted into range constants (1, 2, 3, . . .). A probable estimate of once in 100 days would be assigned a range constant of 4 and a cost/loss multiplier constant (P_L) of 3.65. The appropriate use, application, and benefit of each of these

TABLE 9.1   Probability Range Table

Subjective Frequency Time	Value (P)	Annualized Per Year	Loss Multiplier (P_L)
Once in 300 years	1	1/300	.00333
Once in 30 years	2	1/30	.03333
Once in 3 years	3	1/3	.33333
Once in 100 days	4	365/100	3.6500
Once in 10 days	5	365/10	36.500
Once per day	6	365/1	365.00
10 Times per day	7	365/.1	3650.0
100 Times per day	8	365/.01	36500.0

types of constants will be illustrated in the following sections on risk-value methods 1 and 2.

ASSIGNING COST VALUES

One must always ask in a risk analysis what the most *appropriate* cost is to assign to the identified exposure. The physical cost of the resource may definitely not be the most appropriate cost to assign. For example, a disk pack costs $350. The information on the disk may be of far greater value than $350. Therefore, the most appropriate cost is $350 if the exposure was only to an erased (scratched) disk pack. This illustrates that THE EXPOSURES MUST BE DEFINED BEFORE ANY ASSIGNMENT OF COST (LOSS) VALUES!

An aid in selecting the most appropriate cost for each defined exposure is to ask which of the following six types of cost (loss) best matches the defined exposure:

1. The physical cost of the asset.
2. The cost to repair the asset (damage less insurance).
3. The cost to replace the asset (includes ordering, shipping, and installation).
4. The cost to operate without the asset (includes legal loss, delay loss, business confidence loss, opportunity loss).
5. The cost of backup/recovery capability.
6. The cost of insurance.

SUBJECTIVE COST/LOSS VALUES (C)

The cost assigned to a particular resource should also be obtained from the owner or user of the resource. The person most knowledgeable on the worth of the resource should state the most appropriate value to use. That value may be any one of the six types of cost suggested on the previous page. This value or cost should *not* be expressed in terms as specific as, say, $413.20, but rather to the closest multiple of 10 (i.e., $10, $100, $1,000, $10,000, and so on). For example, the accidental destruction of an Accounts Payable file may be assessed by the comptroller as approximately $20,000. Whether it actually is $17,750 or $23,990 is immaterial. The *ballpark* estimate by the owner or user is fully acceptable and usable to meet our ranking objective.

The subjective cost/loss values are also converted into value constants through the use of range tables for ease in calculating risk (R). Table 9.2 presents a range table for performing this conversion. The value constant is directly selected by the positional fit of the cost/loss value. For example, the Accounts Payable file cost/loss estimate of $20,000 made by the comptroller would lie in the table range of $10,000 to $100,000, having the range constant value (C) of 5.

DELPHI TECHNIQUE

It is sometimes difficult to get a consensus on the appropriate cost or probability value assignment. In such cases, the use of a technique known as Delphi[3] may be most helpful. The Delphi technique is a systematic procedure for obtaining the opinions and a possible consensus from a panel of experts on a particular subject.

Originally designed by the RAND Corporation as a vehicle for anonymous debate, the technique is currently used by hundreds of United States corporations. For example, McDonnell Douglas has used Delphi to forecast the future of commercial air transportation; Weyerhaeuser used it to focus on what is going to happen in the construction business; Smith, Kline & French studied the long-range future of medicine; and the National Industrial Conference Board used a Delphi panel in 1975 to capture agreement on the nation's most critical

---

[3]For extensive discussion of the Delphi procedures, see Norman C. Dalkey, *Delphi*, P-3704, RAND Corporation, Santa Monica, California, October 1967, and *The Delphi Method: An Experimental Study of Group Opinion*, RM-5888-PR, RAND Corporation, Santa Monica, California, June 1969, 79 pp.

TABLE 9.2   Cost/Loss Range
Table

Subjective Cost ($)	Constant Value (C)
0 – 10	1
10 – 100	2
100 – 1K	3
1K – 10K	4
10K – 100K	5
100K – 1M	6
1M – 10M	7
10M – 100M	8

problems over the next twenty years. A panel of RAND experts in 1963 used Delphi to predict the scientific breakthroughs anticipated in the future. Their predictions are presented in Table 9.3.

Very simply, the technique as applied in a data security study would be as follows:

1. A cost/loss value for a defined exposure of "power interruption" to the main computer needs to be quantified.

2. Each expert (owner, user) on that topic is asked to submit a written, sealed estimate stating why they chose the value they submitted.

3. An intermediary collects all the estimates and then tallies the results. For example, the range of responses may vary between $10,000 and $1,000,000.

4. All supporting statements are typed without personal reference (anonymously) into a list, which is distributed back to each expert (owner, user) with a copy of the tally.

5. The tally is broken into quartiles—that is, equal fourths of participant responses. For example, in the first trial, out of 30 participants, five estimates were between $10K and $25K and five were between $600K and $1M. The remaining ten estimates lie within an interquartile range of $25K to $600K.

6. A second round is now conducted. Every respondent who revised estimate falls *outside* the interquartile range must briefly state why he or she thought the cost would be much less or more than the majority believe.

7. Four rounds of estimates are conducted in total. Each round provides an anonymous debate on the facts and opinions supporting

TABLE 9.3   Scientific Breakthroughs Predicted by Delphi Panel

Rand scientists   A 1963 panel gave a range of dates when
peer into the future   scientific breakthroughs would be achieved:

Three-fourths by this date

One-half by this date

One-fourth thought by this date

	One-fourth thought by this date	One-half by this date	Three-fourths by this date
Economical desalination of sea water	1964	1970	1980
Ultra-light synthetic construction materials	1970	1971	1978
Automated language translators	1968	1972	1976
New organs through transplanting or prosthesis	1968	1972	1982
Reliable weather forecasts	1972	1975	1988
Wide-access central data storage facility	1971	1979–80	1991
Reformation of physical theory	1975	1980	1993
Implanted plastic or electronic organs	1975	1982	1988
Popular use of personality control drugs	1980	1983	2000
Lasers in X and Gamma ray spectrum region	1978	1985	1989
Controlled thermonuclear power	1980	1986–87	2000
Creation of primitive form of artificial life	1979	1989	2000
Economical ocean-floor mining [other than off-shore drilling]	1980	1989	2000
Limited weather control	1987	1990	2000
Commercial production of synthetic protein for food	1985	1990	2003
Greatly improved physical or chemical therapy for psychotics	1983	1992	2017
General immunization against bacterial and viral diseases	1983	1994	2000
Chemical control over some hereditary defects	1990	2000	2010
Producing 20% of the world's food by ocean farming	2000 –	2000	2017
Growth of new organs and limbs through biochemical stimulation	1995	2007	2040
Using drugs to raise intelligence level	1984	2012	2050

Direct electromechanical interaction between man's brain and computer	1990	2020	3000 +
Extending life span 50 years by chemical control of aging	1995	2050	2070
Breeding intelligent animals for low-grade labor	2020	2040	3000 +
Two-way communication with extra-terrestrials	2000	2075	3000 +
Commercial manufacture of chemical elements from subatomic building blocks	2007	2100	3000 +
Control of gravity	2035	2050	3000 +
Direct information recording on brain	1997	2600	3000 +
Long-duration coma for time travel	2006	3000 +	3000 +
Use of telepathy and ESP in communications	2040	3000 +	3000 +

Reprinted from the March 14, 1970 issue of *Business Week* by special permission, © 1970 by McGraw-Hill, Inc., New York, NY 10020. All rights reserved.

each expert's estimate that continues to lie outside the reconstructed interquartile range.

8. A curve is generated, which may skew up or down in successive rounds as the range narrows. At the end of the fourth round, the median (halfway point) is nominated the consensus opinion. Figure 9.1 graphically portrays what may have occurred.

Many shortcuts and adaptations can be applied to this technique. Any redesign that permits a consensus in minimum time without coercion, threat, intimidation, or the like is the one to use.

Two methods are now presented for the next step in data security analysis. That step is the calculating of risk, or risk analysis. Method 1 is representative of the approach outlined in FIPS Publication 65 mentioned earlier.[4] Method 2 is an adaptation of Dr. Jerry FitzGerald's modification of method 1.

RISK VALUE—METHOD 1

The assessment of risk (R) is developed for each defined exposure at each control point location. For example, in Chapter 7, Figure 7.4, an A1 exposure was defined at CP1 for the accidental disclosure of payroll

[4]See fn. 2.

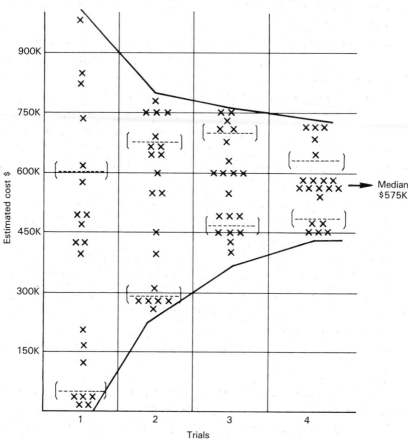

Figure 9.1

data. If the comptroller believed an interruption of the employee would occur four times a year with a potential cost/loss of $15,000, the *P* constant from Table 9.1 would be 4 and the *C* constant from Table 9.2 would be 5. Applying these constant values in Table 9.4 provides a direct risk assessment for this exposure of $300,000. Therefore, the expected cost/loss of an accidentally disclosed payroll timesheet at CP1 (data gathering) is approximately $300,000/year.

Table 9.4 is derived by using the following expression:

$$R = \frac{10^{P-3}}{3} \times 10^{C}$$

TABLE 9.4   (R) Risk Value Table

		P, Probability Value Constants							
C, Cost/Loss Value Constants		Once/300 Years (100,000 Days)	Once/30 Years (10,000 Days)	Once/3 Years (1,000 Days)	Once/100 Days	Once/10 Days	Once/ Day	10 Times/ Day	100 Times/ Day
		1	2	3	4	5	6	7	8
0–10	1	–	–	**3**	**30**	300	3K	30K	300K
10–100	2	–	**3**	**30**	300	3K	30K	300K	3M
100–1K	3	**3**	**30**	300	3K	30K	300K	3M	30M
1K–10K	4	**30**	300	3K	30K	300K	3M	30M	300M
10K–100K	5	300	3K	30K	300K	3M	30M	300M	**3B**
100K–1M	6	3K	30K	300K	3M	30M	300M	**3B**	**30B**
1M–10M	7	30K	300K	3M	30M	300M	**3B**	**30B**	**300B**
10M–100M	8	300K	3M	30M	300M	**3B**	**30B**	**300B**	3T

Notes: P = probability (frequency) of occurrence

C = cost/loss assigned to exposure

K = 1,000; M = million; B = billion; T = trillion dollars

All risk values (R) from the table are rounded to the nearest whole number.

Boldface areas represent either insignificant values or business extremes (losing the business 10 times/day).

91

where $10^{P-3}/3$ is the probability of occurrence/year

$$R = \frac{10^{P+C-3}}{3} = \text{the annual expected \$ cost/loss}$$

If desired, a more complete explanation of the formulation of the table is available in FIPS Publication 65.[5] Table 9.4 simply incorporates the arithmetic mechanics of computation for the user.

RISK ANALYSIS GRID—METHOD 1

The values from Table 9.4 are most appropriately placed in a class level/ exposure risk grid as shown in Table 9.5. For example, exposure A1 displays the risk value developed for accidentally disclosing payroll data. The value of \$300K is, therefore, placed in the risk exposure box at CP1 for exposure A1. Each identified data exposure A1 through F(n) is listed and its corresponding risk value posted in the appropriate (R) box.

The matrix grid is then viewed for the highest risk value (R) obtained for any exposure listed. This value is classified as type "A" risk. In Table 9.5, the highest risk value is \$30 million. Therefore, \$30 million is classified as the type "A" risk value. The next greatest risk value, \$3 million, is classified type "B," and so on.

Each exposure is so classified across all control points, revealing the locations of greatest risk. For example, the matrix in Table 9.5 shows that exposure A1 (accidental disclosure of a particular resource) at CP10 (data usage) is a class "A" risk. Exposure A4 at CP1 also has a class "A" risk level.

At this point, all risks are quantified and classified as to priority of dollar cost/loss. We can now focus on controlling these most critical risks. Limited resources can be appropriately applied to the areas of greatest exposure risk. The system is ready for effective control considerations.

RISK VALUE—METHOD 2

The second method for calculating risk employs the use of cost/loss multipliers. Fractional equivalents of time periods are used in place of assigned constants. These values (P_L) are provided in Table 9.1 simply by converting each time period into its *yearly* fractional equivalent. If de-

[5]Ibid.

TABLE 9.5　Class Level/Exposure Risk Priority Ratings

Identified Data Exposure		Data Exposure Control Points										
		1	2	3	4	5	6	7	8	9	10	11
A1	(R)	300K	30K	30K	30K	3.0	3.0M	30	3.0K	300K	30M	3.0
	CL	C	D	D	D	H	B	G	E	C	A	H
A2	(R)											
	CL						C					
A3	(R)											
	CL	B	B									
A4	(R)											
	CL	A							C	C		
B1	(R)											
	CL			C								E
B2	(R)											
	CL				B	B	A					
C1	(R)											
	CL									A		
	(R)											
	CL			A								
			D									
F(n)	(R)											
	CL		B									

CLASS LEVEL RATING (CL):

A = greatest exposure in $/year

B = next greatest exposure in $/year

C = next greatest

D = etc.

sired, a more complete range of values could be expressed from which to choose, as illustrated in Table 9.6.

The cost/loss value (see the discussion of *ballpark* estimate on p. 86) is multiplied by the cost/loss multiplier found in Table 9.6. There is no need to apply the subjective cost/loss range values. If the accidental destruction of an Accounts Payable file was assessed with a cost/loss

TABLE 9.6   Annualized Cost/Loss
Multiplier Table

Subjective Frequency Time Period	Annualized Fractional Equivalent	Cost/Loss Multiplier (P_L)
Never	—	.0
Once each 200 years	1/200	.005
Once each 100 years	1/100	.01
Once each 50 years	1/50	.02
Once each 25 years	1/25	.04
Once each 5 years	1/5	.20
Once each 2 years	1/2	.50
Once each year	1	1.00
Twice a year	1/.5	2.00
Four times a year	1/.25	4.00
Once each month	12/1	12.00
Twice a month	12/.5	24.00
Once each week	52/1	52.00
Once each day	365/1	365.0
Twice each day	365/.5	730.0
Ten times a day	365/.1	3,650.0
Once an hour	8,760/1	8,760.0
Twice an hour	8,760/.5	17,520.0

value of $20,000, then $20,000 would be the value used in the calculation. For example, if the same file had a probability of being destroyed once every two years, then the annualized cost/loss multiplier (P_L) from Table 9.6 of .5 would be multiplied times $20,000, resulting in an overall risk assessment of $10,000.

Both the first and second methods of approach may be applied as a direct follow-on to the methodology presented in Chapter 7. The two preceding sections outlined a follow-on using method 1. Method 2 may be illustrated by using the same example presented in the first of those sections. For example, the comptroller's estimate of a potential cost/loss value of $15,000 for the accidental disclosure of payroll data at CP1 is multiplied by the cost/loss multiplier (P_L) value, 4.0, representing a probability of occurrence four times per year. The result is a risk assessment value of $60,000. Notice that this value is considerably less than the $300,000 assessed by method 1.

Remember, method 1's strength was the ease of use (by all parties involved) for ranking exposures in minimum time. It achieved this objective by using gross numerical value multiples (power of 10) within ranges. The result was a discernible spread or separation between exposure risks, as illustrated in Table 9.5. This adequate separation in values was key to the classification of risk for each exposure.

Method 2 does not provide as wide a value spread between exposures. It requires computational effort and closer scrutiny to assess and classify each exposure's risk. However, method 2 does afford the practitioner a better assessment of risk values by using more definitive estimates (actual cost/loss value) in place of ranges. The strength of method 2 is the development of a set of risk values usable for a cost-effectiveness study as presented in Chapter 10. Therefore, this method is recommended to the analyst who desires to do more than define controls for each critical exposure. This technique provides a follow-on to the methodology from performance of a risk analysis to developing the most cost-effective set of controls for the existing exposures.

Tables 9.7 and 9.8 represent the workpapers for evaluating risk and rating exposures using method 2. Note the similarity to, yet difference from, method 1's display in Table 9.5! First, the risks are derived from the actual cost/loss estimate (C/L) multiplied by the probability of occurrence (P_L) instead of the selection of a value range table. Therefore, the identified data exposure "A1," at CP1, receives a risk assessment of $60K in Table 9.8. The identical point in Table 9.5 was assessed at $300K. A similar experience occurs across all data exposure control points.

Second, the class level ratings are very similar by groupings, yet, method 2 affords the property of distinction between groups. For example, Table 9.5 classified the highest dollar exposure risk as a class "A." This dollar value was $30 million. The next highest value of $3.0 million was classified as class "B." In contrast, Table 9.8's values are all distinctive; i.e., most all risk values are different. However, if Table 9.8 assigns priority rankings by value groupings ($3.0 million to $30 million; $300,000 to $3.0 million; $30,000 to $300,000; etc.) within the powers-of-ten range used in Table 9.5, almost all values match. For instance, class 17 in Table 9.8 equals a "C" rating for exposure "A1" at CP1. Table 9.5 also classifies this as a "C." Also, class 4 in Table 9.8 equals an "A" rating for exposure "B2" at CP6. Table 9.5 also classifies this as an "A."

SUMMARY

In summary, method 1 offers the practitioner a faster, easier way of quantifying risk values. It requires no calculations, since it uses tables to determine the assigned exposure ratings. In addition, the greatest expo-

Table 9.7   Risk Value Table
(Method 2)

Identified Data Exposure		Data Exposure Control Points										
		1	2	3	4	5	6	7	8	9	10	11
A1	C/L	15K	5K	4K	5K	500	25K	1K	500	20K	35K	100
	P_L	4.0	2.0	2.0	2.0	.005	52	.02	4.0	12	365	.02
A2	C/L						10K					
	P_L						24					
A3	C/L	60K	35K									
	P_L	24	52									
A4	C/L	41K							50K	33K		
	P_L	730							4.0	12		
B1	C/L			18K								50
	P_L			12								4.0
B2	C/L				100K	250K	350K					
	P_L				24	12	52					
C1	C/L									40K		
	P_L									730		
	C/L			2M								
	P_L			12								
		25K										
		1.0										
F(n)	C/L		75K									
	P_L		12									

Table 9.8 Class Level/Exposure Risk Priority Ratings

Identified Data Exposure		Data Exposure Control Points										
		1	2	3	4	5	6	7	8	9	10	11
A1	(R)	60K	10K	8K	10K	2.5	1.3M	20	2K	240K	12.8M	2.0
	CL	17	19	21	20	25	10	24	22	13	5	26
A2	(R)						240K					
	CL						14					
A3	(R)	1.4M	1.8M									
	CL	9	8									
A4	(R)	29.9M							200K	396K		
	CL	1							16	12		
B1	(R)			216K								200
	CL			15								23
B2	(R)				2.4M	3.0M	18.2M					
	CL				7	6	4					
C1	(R)									29.2M		
	CL									2		
	(R)			24M								
	CL			3								
				25K								
				18								
F(n)	(R)			900K								
	CL			11								

CLASS LEVEL RATING (CL):

A = (CLs 1–5) greatest exposures
    In $/year
B = (CLs 6–12) next greatest
C = (CLs 13–17) next greatest
D = etc. (CLs 18–21)

sure risks are most obvious by the sheer magnitude of values assigned. $30 million is noticeably different from $3M, $300K, $30K, and so on.

On the other hand, method 2's calculations are not difficult and result in assigning each identified exposure an individual risk value. Although the risk value spread is much closer, the exposures can be rated in a definite priority sequence: 1, 2, 3, and so on. Furthermore, method 2 offers the practitioner the capability to continue forward with a set of meaningful values for use in a cost-effectiveness analysis.

The values of risk derived in Tables 9.5 and 9.7 are highly inflated! This condition exists because an assumption was made that absolutely no controls presently exist in the organization that could affect the exposures identified in the system. This is a highly unrealistic assumption, used only as an extreme case for purposes of illustration and example. Obviously, when the practitioner assesses the risk in the information system under study, the controls already available in the organization will mitigate the cost/loss. The result will be assigned values of much less magnitude, representing the actual condition.

Furthermore, it is important to understand that each of the control points studied represents an independent event. A total information loss could occur at each control point. If this loss would shut the doors of the business, it is possible to have a grand total greater than ten times the value of the business. Therefore, *the values of risk are not additive in representing a total system loss!* They represent only potential cost/loss for each exposure. This fact does *not* degrade the use of this technique for performing a risk analysis. The basic objectives are still met.

Both methods 1 and 2 meet the basic objectives of a risk analysis. They aid in the identification of exposures and permit the ranking of exposures by priority. Attention can now be focused on these prime-high risk exposures for the consideration of control. The practitioner's next step is to view all the possible controls available to limit these exposure costs to the system and thus to the business.

10

BASIC CONTROLS

CONTROL DEFINED

Control is the capability to exercise restraint or direct influence over a given situation or event. It is an action taken to make an event conform to plan. Some controls are passive in nature; others are active. That is, some controls require no feedback before a planned action is taken. For example, a key is turned in a lock and the door opens; or an order is entered and the control system automatically stamps it with date and time of entry. No other considerations or actions are necessary for initiating and maintaining this type of control. Others are quite active and require feedback for proper operation. For example, a thermostat is a control device that takes action to heat or cool a room. The device may be set to any planned temperature. However, control can take place only when the thermostat (controller) is able to actively compare what was planned with what is actual.

Some controls in DP function much like the thermostat. They are designed to operate in a particular manner, depending on the conditions present at the moment. A *password* is an active control. It requires comparison to an established authorized code before a planned action is taken. This action may be to permit entry, prevent entry, detect entry or even take corrective action against such entry.

In DP systems, both active and passive types of controls must be used for effective reduction or elimination of data exposures. Controls are used wherever applicable. In DP systems, this includes input, process, output, security, environment, administration, hardware, software, and so on. There are literally thousands of control uses.

PASSWORDS

One of the most common types of data security controls is the password. Passwords may be user-generated or system-generated. Each approach has definite pros and cons that must be examined by the practitioner. Generally, as the number of users and the necessity for frequent change increase, the use of system-generated passwords is favored. However, many users today generate their own passwords. The key factor in a decision of this nature is the ease of password distribution, maintenance, and control. One must select the approach that works best in a particular process of doing business. Which is best? It all depends![1]

IBM has been using system-generated passwords in its administrative system. The latest security code has a five-character alphanumeric format. Previous code schemes worked much as follows: Users of this system must first *key* their employee number and their assigned security code (an alpha, no vowel) password for complete user identification. The elimination of vowels prevents the generation of embarrassing password names. The system checks employee number and security code as follows:

- If employee number is valid and the password is correct, a user is permitted access to the data base.
- If either the employee number or security code does not pass, the event is logged for later review and the user is requested to try again.

Three unsuccessful attempts to access the system will lock the terminal and alert the local security administrator.

A new security code is mailed to each user through a computer generated self-mailer as shown at the top of Figure 10.1. The security code is on a detachable card stub with no other reference data. The receiver is instructed to immediately detach the code stub. Should the user now lose this stub, the finder would have great difficulty in associating the password number with the appropriate system and employee number.

[1]See Dennis K. Branstad, Ph.D., "Password Usage Guidelines," Revised Draft, National Bureau of Standards, Washington, D.C. 20234.

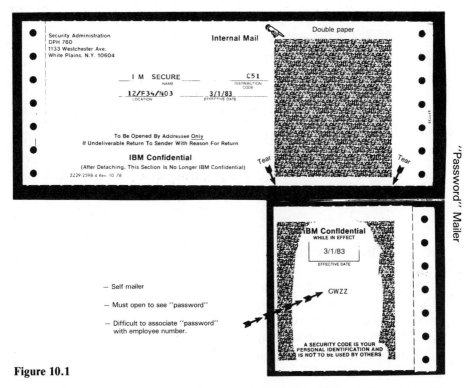

Figure 10.1

If the user suspects his code has been compromised (for example, someone looked over his shoulder at the display upon key entry), he can request a new code at any time. This technique is normally successful in protecting a system from any unauthorized terminal users.

However, *passwords will usually keep out only the casual intruder, not the one who is determined!*

Therefore, additional controls are necessary for securing sensitive data.

PROBLEM AND SOLUTION

A major mistake in approaching controls is to view them too generally, attempting to pick and choose from a massive potpourri in hopes of selecting something adequate for the system. Often the designer does not even understand the control selected. An "anticipation" control used by audit, for example, may be completely foreign to the design engineer.

What is suggested, and can be put into practice immediately with very positive results, is the classification of controls by their basic purpose. Controls serve three basic purposes:

1. To PREVENT the causes of data exposure.
2. To DETECT the causes of data exposure.
3. To CORRECT the causes of data exposure activity.

All the various areas in a system where controls may be used fit into these basic purposes. Combinations of controls will dictate the adequacy achieved.

This approach is often referred to as the three-layer, ring, or barrier concept. Preventive measures form the outermost, or first, layer of protection to the system. These are followed by detective measures and then a layer of corrective actions.

PREVENTIVE CONTROLS

All data is susceptible to influence from threats (undesirable things) existing in its environment. Chapter 5 describes many of these undesirable things. Preventive controls offer the first line of defense or barrier against the bad things that could happen to a data asset. They stop the majority of causal agents from accidentally or intentionally disclosing, modifying, or destroying the data asset. Figure 10.2 illustrates this concept.

Preventive controls are a before-the-fact type of control. Recognition is given that particular causal agents exist, and certain preplanned preventive measures are employed to reduce, if not eliminate, their effect on the data asset. Unfortunately, as illustrated in Figure 10.2, no control or set of controls are perfect in themselves. Therefore, some causal agents will still pose a threat to the data asset after the preventive barrier is established. The purpose of the first control layer, then, is to substantially reduce the number of existing undesirable things in the neighborhood of the data asset. The few bad things that filter through the preventive barrier should be detected and corrected by the second and third layers of control.

Preventive controls generally have the following characteristics: they

1. Are passive, requiring no feedback
   • Lock on a terminal
   • Power-off switch

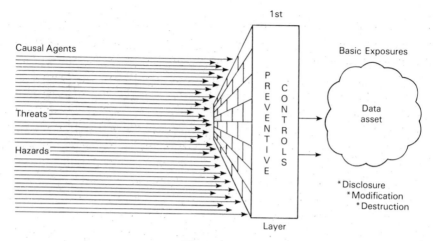

Figure 10.2

- Preset timer
- Fence

2. Guide, to align things to happen correctly
   - Machine feed guides
   - Forms design; formatted coding sheets
   - Training program

3. Are inadequate alone, overlooking a certain percentage of violations
   - No admittance sign
   - Timelock (in/out by others)
   - Automatic door close (prop open)

4. Reduce threat frequency
   - Computer facility inspection
   - Audit
   - Personnel background check
   - Segregation of duties

5. Are transparent; people are not conscious of their existence
   - Fire-retardant furnishings
   - Shatterproof glass
   - Encapsulated circuits

6. Are inexpensive
   - Door lock
   - Cover over an emergency button
   - Badge

DETECTIVE CONTROLS

Detective controls offer the second line of defense against causal agents
that penetrate the preventive barrier. Since the bad thing has happened,
these controls are an after-the-fact type. They are designed specifically
to detect the presence of a causal agent. Figure 10.3 illustrates this
concept.

An interesting aspect of detective controls is that they are seldom
effective by themselves. They note an occurrence. However, unless some
corrective action is taken, the potential for data exposure continues. Detective controls generally have the following characteristics: they

1. Trigger an alarm
   - Smoke detector
   - Voltmeter power-supply warning light
   - Beeper on an opened door
2. Register the threat occurrence
   - Printout of happenings
   - Automatic error counter
   - Photographing of intruder
3. Terminate further system operation
   - Shut down the computer
   - Lock the terminal
   - *Abend* (create an abnormal ending to) a program
4. Monitor occurrence and range of acceptance

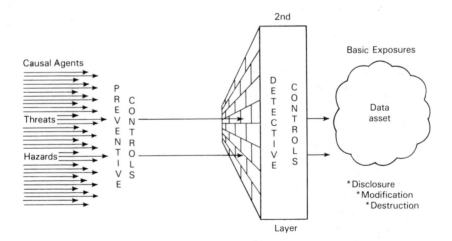

Figure 10.3

- Reasonableness checks (aspirin @ $1,000/tablet)
- Anticipation of an event (sign-on time)
- Tolerance level (200V–240V)
5. Alert personnel
   - Siren, horn, buzzer
   - Warning, flashing light
   - Error reports
   - Debug routines with diagnostics
6. Test preventive control operation
   - Hash totals, check digits
   - Balancing of control totals
   - Reconciliation of accounts

CORRECTIVE CONTROLS

Corrective controls are generally paired with detective controls. Once the penetration has occurred and is noted, a corrective action for that causal agent is executed. The purpose of the corrective control is to take action on righting a wrong or preventing more wrongs from occurring. Figure 10.4 illustrates this concept.

Many corrective controls are of the management type; that is, they require stated policies, procedures, and programs for execution. Corrective controls generally have the following characteristics: they

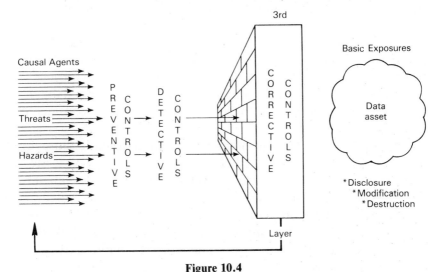

Figure 10.4

1. Take action to resolve a problem
   - Automatic error correction (refuse overdraw)
   - Graceful degradation (slow shutdown)
   - Exception management (EOQ point: automatic reorder)
2. Reset for reprocess
   - Corrected rejects resubmitted upstream
   - Approved exceptions returned to entry point
3. Are expensive
   - Parallel operation
   - Backup/recovery resources
   - Change control center
   - Quality control group
4. Provide investigative assist
   - Audit trail
   - Discrepancy report

A more comprehensive list of examples of these three types of controls is presented in Appendix C.

SELECTING CONTROLS

It is obvious that the data asset may be vulnerable to (susceptible to influence by) an infinite number of possible causal agents (threats, hazards) in its environment. Trying to consider controls for each of these undesirable things would be very difficult if not impractical. Although that approach may be viewed as the classical method, it is as absurd as the listing of all possible exposures. Fortunately, in the identification of exposures presented in Chapter 5, a technique was developed that limits the number of exposures and their causes that need to be considered for purposes of control.

Figure 7.4 illustrates this point by describing the basic causes of the identified data exposures at CP1. For example, exposure A1 is the accidental disclosure of a timesheet caused by an employee's leaving it unattended on his desk. The consideration of basic controls is limited to that specific cause. Therefore, controls are considered not for the mass of possible causal agents but *only* for the specific causes described in the process of identifying exposures. This greatly simplifies the control problem and, as a result, reduces the time required to complete the control process. An effective approach to designing or assessing controls for causes of data exposure is now available for use.

Figure 10.5 illustrates a workpaper that may be used to facilitate the process of deriving and recording control data for each exposure at each control point. The user of the form enters:

1. Proper date, system studied, control point examined, basic data exposure defined.
2. Description of the type and nature of controls (considered as a "set") to apply the specific threat causing the exposure.
3. An annualized cost of the recommended control or control set. (*Note:* The actual cost of the control is the cost of both installation and operation. The installation charge is generally amortized over the life of the asset involved. For example, if the control in question were the use of an electronic scanner or camera, the installation charge would be amortized over five years. Most computers and small electronic equipment (not used for R & D) are recognized by the IRS as having a five-year capital cost recovery period. The operational charge per year is then added to this amount. The total, Cc, represents the annualized cost of the control or control set.)
4. The probability that the defined control (set) will successfully eliminate this specific threat for this basic exposure.

The information captured on the form in Figure 10.5 may come from several sources. The selected controls may be a designer input, quality assurance presentation, user idea, auditor recommendation, or risk assessment team's suggestion. However, the person or persons most familiar and/or involved with the particular exposure under examination should be called upon to:

1. Suggest their thoughts.
2. Estimate the probability of success associated with such controls.
3. Express an annualized "ballpark" cost of the control set.

Warning: Do *not* try to be exact at this point! The values given should be best educated guesses. This is sufficient to provide the input necessary for further analysis. Even-numbered percentages of 10, 20, 30, . . ., up to 100 and costs of 1, 10, 100, . . ., in multiples of 10,000 are suggested.

Figure 10.6 is an illustration of a completed control set for one of the defined data exposures at CP1.

Control Set Workpaper

Date: __1.__   System: ___1.___

Control point: __1.__   Data exposure: __1.__ (Basic)

P(s):   __4.__   Probability of this control set successfully
                       eliminating the data exposure.

*C(c):   __3.__   Annualized cost of this control set.

Selected controls: (Preventive, detective, corrective)

2.

*Expressed in the following 'multiples':   Negligible (about $1)
                                              On the order of $10
                                              On the order of $100
                                              On the order of $1,000
                                              On the order of $10,000
                                              On the order of $20,000
                                              Continue multiples of $10,000

Figure 10.5

Control Set Workpaper

Date: July 1, 1982   System: Payroll

Control point: 1   Data exposure: C1 (Basic)

P(s): .90   Probability of this control set successfully eliminating the data exposure.

*C(c): $1,000   Annualized cost of this control set.

Selected controls: (Preventive, detective, corrective)

P — Pressure clips will be installed on the sides of each card rack to hold the cards firmly in place at all times.

P — Cards will be returned to the supervisor for filing (separation of duties and responsibilities).

D — The slot from which the card is pulled, when exposed, will be highly visible (painted bright red) as an open box.

C — A training session will be held periodically to alert the employees to the continued need for care in card movement. It is suggested that this would become part of a total awareness program. The penalty of immediate dismissal for any incident of a fraudulant nature would be emphasized!

*Expressed in the following 'multiples':   Negligible (about $1)
On the order of $10
On the order of $100
On the order of $1,000
On the order of $10,000
On the order of $20,000
Continue multiples of $10,000

Figure 10.6

INSURANCE

Insurance may also be regarded by some people as a control. However, insurance is a means of recovering from a loss rather than preventing, detecting, or correcting a loss. Potential causes of loss are unaffected. Therefore, insurance will be considered only as a backup to the control measures that are adopted.

SOFTWARE CONTROLS

Today there is a proliferation of software controls available from many vendors. The designer and auditor may find many of these "canned" software products useful to them in meeting their control needs. The question is, "How are such control packages related to the data security methodology?"

Table 10.1[2] represents a tool for identifying the specific controls by type and function and then relating them to the applicable data exposure control points. Tables 10.2 through 10.6 show how this tool would be used in terms of a number of data security products offered in 1982 by the IBM Corporation. The degree of control provided by each product feature varies widely from a "token" effort to total protectiveness and can be determined only by a *thorough* understanding of the package. In assessing the control value of software, therefore, one may find it helpful to place some quantitative value (1 through 10) rather than a dot in each affected position.

[2]Designed by Rudy Van Loon, Institute Staff Member, Chicago Information Systems Management Institute, IBM Corporation.

TABLE 10.1 IBM Products Data Security Features

Product	Control/Feature	Type			Functions						Applicable Data Exposure Control Points											
		Preventive	Detective	Corrective	Identification	Authentication	Authorization	Delegation	Audit Trail	Surveillance	1	2	3	4	5	6	7	8	9	10	11

TABLE 10.2 IBM Products Data Security Features (Current as of 8/82)

Product	Control/Feature	Type			Functions						Applicable Data Exposure Control Points										
		Preventive	Detective	Corrective	Identification	Authentication	Authorization	Delegation	Audit Trail	Surveillance	1	2	3	4	5	6	7	8	9	10	11
OS/VS2 (MVS)	1. System integrity: Reference IBM Programming Announcement dated 4/21/80.	●	●	●	●	●	●	●	●	●		●	●	●	●	●	●		●		
	2. Store/Fetch protection	●					●									●					
	3. High integrity user-to-user, user-to-system isolation	●	●		●	●	●		●							●	●				
	4. Authorized program facility	●					●	●								●					
	5. Password protection for datasets	●					●								●	●	●				
	6. System Management Facility (SMF) log—Journals dataset accesses, naming/renaming, job runs—protected by MVS—utilized by authorized subsystems		●	●			●		●	●					●	●	●				

TABLE 10.3 IBM Products Data Security Features (Current as of 8/82)

Product	Control/Feature	Type			Functions						Applicable Data Exposure Control Points										
		Preventive	Detective	Corrective	Identification	Authentication	Authorization	Delegation	Audit Trail	Surveillance	1	2	3	4	5	6	7	8	9	10	11
OS/VS2 (MVS) <u>TSO</u>	1. User identification and authentication via password	●			●	●							●	●		●			●		
	2. Session data logged to SMF		●						●	●						●					
	3. Account command for delegation control	●						●								●					

113

TABLE 10.4 IBM Products Data Security Features (Current as of 8/82)

Product	Control/Feature	Type			Functions						Applicable Data Exposure Control Points										
		Preventive	Detective	Corrective	Identification	Authentication	Authorization	Delegation	Audit Trail	Surveillance	1	2	3	4	5	6	7	8	9	10	11
OS/VS2 (MVS) VSAM	1. Password control of VSAM datasets and catalog	●					●								●	●	●				
	2. Exits for journaling and exception processing		●	●			●		●	●					●	●	●				
	3. Hierarchy of password levels for control	●					●	●							●	●	●				
	4. Dataset sharing control	●					●									●					
	5. Erase option allowing deleted data to be overwritten with binary zeros	●					●									●					

TABLE 10.5 IBM Products Data Security Features (Current as of 8/82)

Product	Control/Feature	Preventive	Detective	Corrective	Identification	Authentication	Authorization	Delegation	Audit Trail	Surveillance	1	2	3	4	5	6	7	8	9	10	11
						Functions								Applicable Data Exposure Control Points							
VM/370	1. Extensive user-to-user and user-to-control-program isolation in individual virtual machines	●	●		●	●	●		●							●	●				
	2. User identification and authentication by user-ID and password	●			●	●							●	●		●			●		
	3. Journaling of unsuccessful attempts to LOGON or LINK		●	●					●	●			●			●			●		
	4. Installation defined threshold for journaling unsuccessful attempts	●	●						●	●						●					
	5. Notification of system administrator unsuccessful attempts		●	●					●	●			●			●			●		
	6. Password Print/Display suppression. For CMS and Minidisk passwords	●				●	●						●			●			●		
	7. Read inhibit support for virtual machines to suppress security information printing	●				●	●						●			●			●		
	8. Authority delegation by system administrator by use of operator authorization class	●					●	●								●					

115

TABLE 10.6 IBM Products Data Security Features (Current as of 8/82)

Product	Control/Feature	Preventive	Detective	Corrective	Identification	Authentication	Authorization	Delegation	Audit Trail	Surveillance	1	2	3	4	5	6	7	8	9	10	11
						Type			Functions					Applicable Data Exposure Control Points							
DOS/VSE	1. IPL user exit—user-supplied code to perform integrity and security checks	●	●		●	●	●									●					
	2. Job control user exit—user-supplied code to perform various access control checks	●	●	●	●	●	●		●	●					●	●	●				
	3. Standard file labeling—file name, retention period, expiration date	●	●				●								●	●	●				
	4. Data secured files—console warning message, operator decision	●					●	●	●	●					●	●	●				
	5. DASD file protection—prevents program access to data outside file limits	●		●			●								●	●	●				
	6. Reliability data extractor records reason for IPL		●						●	●						●					
VSE/Power 5746-XE7	1. Reader user exit—user-supplied checks for security and resource access	●	●	●	●	●	●		●	●					●	●	●		●		
	2. RJE user identification and passwords check at SIGNON/LOGON	●			●	●							●	●		●			●		

TABLE 10.7 IBM Products Data Security Features (Current as of 8/82)

Product	Control/Feature	Type			Functions						Applicable Data Exposure Control Points										
		Preventive	Detective	Corrective	Identification	Authentication	Authorization	Delegation	Audit Trail	Surveillance	1	2	3	4	5	6	7	8	9	10	11
DOS/VSE VSE/VSAM	1. Access authorization Passwords - Read PW - Update PW - Control PW - Master PW	●					●								●	●	●				
	2. User security verification routine—user-written authorization checks	●		●			●								●	●	●				
	3. Erase parameter—data overwritten with binary zeros when deleted	●					●									●					

TABLE 10.8 IBM Products Data Security Features (Current as of 8/82)

Product	Control/Feature	Type			Functions						Applicable Data Exposure Control Points										
		Preventive	Detective	Corrective	Identification	Authentication	Authorization	Delegation	Audit Trail	Surveillance	1	2	3	4	5	6	7	8	9	10	11
DOS/VSE VSE/ICCF 5746-TS1	*Interactive Computing and Control Facility*																				
	1. User profiles containing user-ID, log-on password, security class	●			●	●	●						●			●			●		
	2. Access authorization to libraries and data	●					●								●	●	●				
	3. Library member password	●					●								●	●	●				
	4. Data protection tables —System program table —Authorized programs —Load protection table —Load/Fetch protection —System file table —Disk volumes and files	●					●								●	●	●				
VSE/Access Control Logging & Reporting 5746-XE7	1. Logging and monitoring access to files, libraries, and programs to log files		●	●					●	●			●	●	●	●	●		●		
	2. Reporting module to produce access control reports from log data sets		●	●				●	●	●			●	●	●	●	●		●		

118

TABLE 10.9 IBM Products Data Security Features (Current as of 8/82)

Product	Control/Feature	Type			Functions						Applicable Data Exposure Control Points										
		Preventive	Detective	Corrective	Identification	Authentication	Authorization	Delegation	Audit Trail	Surveillance	1	2	3	4	5	6	7	8	9	10	11
ACF/VTAM 5746-RC3 (DOS/VS) 5735-RCZ (OS/VS)	1. SNA terminal identification verification on switched lines	●			●	●							●	●					●		
	2. BSC and TWX identification verification on switched lines	●			●	●							●	●					●		
	3. Authorization exit routine (user written)	●	●		●	●	●	●	●	●			●	●		●			●		
	4. Log-on exit in application program	●	●	●			●	●	●	●			●	●		●			●		
	5. Control of application access to ACF/VTAM and selected ACF/VTAM facilities	●					●									●					
	6. Protection of confidential data in ACF/VTAM buffers	●					●									●					
	7. Message sequence numbering		●	●					●					●					●		
	8. Message counts by terminal		●	●					●					●					●		

TABLE 10.10 IBM Products Data Security Features (Current as of 8/82)

Product	Control/Feature	Type — Preventive	Type — Detective	Type — Corrective	Functions — Identification	Functions — Authentication	Functions — Authorization	Functions — Delegation	Functions — Audit Trail	Functions — Surveillance	Applicable Data Exposure Control Points
VSPC 5746-XR3 (DOS/VS) 5740-XR5 (VS/1) 5740-XR6 (MVS)	*Virtual Storage Personal Computing*										1 2 3 4 5 6 7 8 9 10 11
	1. High integrity user-to-user and user-to-system isolation	●	●		●		●		●		6, 9
	2. User identification and authentication checking via password	●			●	●					
	3. Access control to procedures and data via user-ID, sharing with lockword	●				●	●	●			3, 6
	4. Realtime, distributed administration		●	●				●			4, 5, 6, 7
	5. Logging of: Variances, administrative activity, system and non-VSAM resource use		●	●						●	●	3, 5, 6, 7, 9

120

TABLE 10.11   IBM Products Data Security Features (Current as of 8/82)

Product	Control/Feature	Type			Functions						Applicable Data Exposure Control Points										
		Preventive	Detective	Corrective	Identification	Authentication	Authorization	Delegation	Audit Trail	Surveillance	1	2	3	4	5	6	7	8	9	10	11
CICS/VS 5740-XX1 (OS/VS) 5746-XX3 (DOS/VS)	1. Transaction (application) security keys verified against user security keys	●			●	●	●				.		●		●	●	●		●		
	2. Exclusive control technique for concurrent data base updating	●					●									●					
	3. Automatic journaling with application access for user code		●	●				●	●	●				●	●	●	●	●	●	●		
	4. Operating statistics available to authorized operator on: transactions, terminals, application programs, CICS/VS files and DL/1 data bases		●	●				●	●	●				●	●	●	●	●		●		

TABLE 10.12 IBM Products Data Security Features (Current as of 8/82)

Product	Control/Feature	Preventive	Detective	Corrective	Identification	Authentication	Authorization	Delegation	Audit Trail	Surveillance	1	2	3	4	5	6	7	8	9	10	11
IMS/VS 5740-XXZ	1. Terminal security—selected transactions entered from specific, designated terminals or systems	●			●	●	●						●		●	●	●		●		
	2. Password security—trans. processed only if password is appended to transaction code	●					●									●					
	3. User exits for security code to provide: —User identification verification at sign on	●			●	●							●	●	●		●		●		
	—Transaction level authorization	●					●									●					
	—Program-to-program switch validation	●					●									●					
	—User ID logged with messages, sign on, sign off, DB changes															●					
	4. Log of all detected security violations —MTO notification of unauthorized access attempts		●	●					●	●			●		●	●	●		●		

Type | Functions | Applicable Data Exposure Control Points

122

5. Logical data structures	●	●		●	
—Controlled application view of physical data		●		●	
6. Data Sensitivity	●	●	●	●	
—Field level sensitivity—logical view of ordered subset of fields in a segment	●	●	●	●	●
	●	●	●	●	
				●	
				●	
7. Access rule authorization of defined sensitive data	●	●	●		
				●	
				●	
					●
8. Log of all messages, SIGNON, SIGNOFF, data base changes				●	●
9. Security maintenance utility				●	●

TABLE 10.13   IBM Products Data Security Features (Current as of 8/82)

Product	Control/Feature	Type: Preventive	Type: Detective	Type: Corrective	Functions: Identification	Functions: Authentication	Functions: Authorization	Functions: Delegation	Functions: Audit Trail	Functions: Surveillance	Applicable Data Exposure Control Points 1	2	3	4	5	6	7	8	9	10	11
RACF (5740-XXH)	*Resource Access Control Facility*																				
	1. User identification and authentication checking —Batch, TSO, IMS/VS users —CICS/VS —Password and/or OID card —Plus many more items	●			●	●							●			●			●		
	2. Authorization checking —*What* a user may access —*How* it can be accessed —For DASD, tape datasets —IMS/VS transactions —CICS/VS transactions —User application datasets	●					●								●	●	●				
	3. Logging to SMF & reporting —All, successful, unsuccessful attempts at use of protected resources, RACF profiles —User option		●	●					●	●			●		●	●	●		●		

4. Unauthorized attempts written immediately to security console

5. Automatic data set protection (ADSP) and user attribute modelling for automatic, dynamic protection [see *Note*]

6. Auditor attribute to oversee entire system

7. Centralized or decentralized control at installation option

8. Extensive tailoring capabilities via user exits

9. Reauthorize option for IMS/VS transactions

10. Individual and group attribute capabilities to facilitate administration

Note: Two different profile types for resources (generic and discrete). Protection implemented explicitly (command instructions) or automatically. Reference: "RACF" General Information Manual GC28-0722.

11

COST-EFFECTIVENESS
SELECTION PROCESS

TRADE-OFF ANALYSIS

Once the exposures and controls are identified and evaluated (i.e., a quantitative value assigned), a trade-off analysis may be performed to determine a hierarchy of effective controls for securing the system. These controls are then presented to management for their consideration. Management now decides on the amount of control cost versus risk they are willing to accept.

This decision by management is based on answers to the following questions: What are the greatest exposures to the system? Which controls affecting these exposures provide the greatest return on investment? What is the expected payback? What overall controls for these exposures are recommended to provide the most effective cost/benefit in protecting data in this system? And, is this risk any greater than that present in other parts of the business not affected by this system?

A cost-effectiveness study is a search for the optimum trade-off point between cost and benefit. The cost in a data security system is the cost of the controls to limit exposure. The benefit is described as the reduction in exposure or cost/loss as a result of using the controls. This relationship between cost of controls and cost/loss as a result of using the controls can be presented graphically as in Figure 11.1. Although the graph is simplistic, it is effective in showing this trade-off relationship.

Optimal Implementation Of Controls

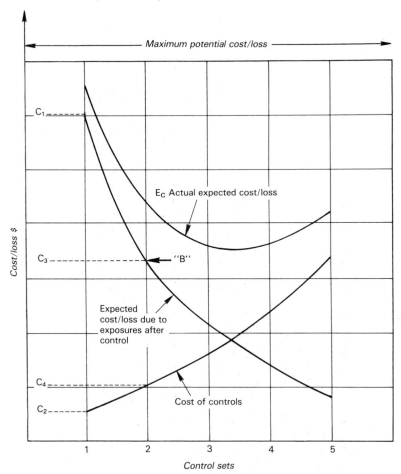

Figure 11.1

For example, zero control exposes the total system. Therefore, the maximum potential cost/loss may be the business itself! Those sets of controls that *provide the greatest reduction of exposure for least cost* are now applied. Control set 1 in Figure 11.1 may be comprised of just one of many types of controls (P, D, C) which reduce the maximum loss to "C1" dollars for a control cost of "C2". Therefore, the actual expected cost is the sum of these two costs—the cost of control and the remaining cost/loss after applying the control. This is reflected in the top curve entitled "actual expected cost/loss."

The next most effective cost/benefit set of controls is set 2. Control set 2 drops the cost/loss (after controls are in place) to point "B" at a value of "C3". The respective cost of control is "C4", which, when added to "C3", gives the actual expected cost/loss, "Ec". Therefore, each control set has two major effects: (1) they reduce the maximum potential loss, and (2) they increase the expected loss by the cost of the controls applied.

As the reduction in exposure cost/loss decreases and the cost of additional controls increases, the actual cost/loss bottoms and then rises again. Figure 11.1 shows that the optimum trade-off exists between applying the third and fourth set of controls. After that, the cost is greater than the added benefit.

APPROACH

The practitioner needs a method for deriving this optimal point range where the controls selected provide the minimum actual expected cost/loss. The trick is to determine those sets of controls that provide the greatest reduction of exposure for the least cost. That is also the objective of a cost-effectiveness study. That is, what is the net effect in the reduction of risk, the avoidance of cost, after the controls are applied? Table 11.1 provides the necessary tool to make this determination.

Table 11.1 draws together the risk assessments of Table 9.8 and the control set workpapers of Figure 10.6 in order to determine the proper selection of system controls. The columns are as follows:

Column 1. Class Rank. All identified exposures are listed in order of risk hierarchy from the greatest to the least.

Column 2. Exposure Identification. A coded brief description is given of the particular basic exposure identified at what location.

Column 3. Risk. The estimated potential risk of cost/loss is expressed in dollars per year.

Column 4. Controls Success. This percentage represents the probability that the controls selected will successfully eliminate the risk.

Column 5. Cost Avoidance. The expected benefit, depending on the success of the controls applied (Column 3 times Column 4).

Column 6. Controls Cost. The total cost in dollars of all the controls used to eliminate this exposure.

TABLE 11.1   Cost-Effectiveness Table Form

\$ Exposure/Class Rank			Selected Control Set Decision						
Class Rank	Exposure Identification/Location	Risk	Ps	Ca	Cc	Net Cost	% ROI	Ce Rank	I
1	2	3	4	5	6	7	8	9	10

Column 7.   Net Cost. This number represents the difference between the cost avoided (Column 5) and the cost of the controls (Column 6).

Column 8.   Return on Investment. The ROI shows, for each dollar spent on controls, what percent return in cost/loss reduction is exected (Column 7/Column 6).

Column 9.   Cost-Effectiveness Ranking. The ROI (Column 8), ranked from highest to lowest (Ce).

Column 10.   Adequacy. Inadequately controlled risks are identified (I).

Table 11.2 is a preview of how Table 11.1 might appear with values. It uses the data from the previous chapters to illustrate the use of this form. Remember, these particular values are highly inflated, owing to the assumption of total absence of *any* controls when the exposure risks were assessed in Tables 9.5 and 9.7. Therefore, both the risk and control values presented in Table 11.2 are extraordinary because of the absolute lack of any basic information system control functions as presented in Chapter 2 (i.e., identification, authentication, authorization, delegation, audit trail, and surveillance). Anyone could interface with this system and be completely unchallenged and undetected. This indeed may be a highly unrealistic assumption (extreme case); however, it is useful as an example to illustrate the application and benefit of Table 11.2 to the practitioner.

ANALYSIS

Column 8 of Table 11.2 presents the actual expected percentage of dollar avoidance in exposure for every dollar expended for controls. Very simply, if $2 worth of controls would avoid $5 of exposure cost/loss, then the ROI on the control set is $5 − $2 = $3 benefit, divided by $2 cost, resulting in an ROI of 150%. Each of the ranked exposures offers an ROI.

The ROIs are ranked in Column 9 by order of best return or cost-effectiveness (Ce). This gives the practitioner a *first* indication of an order of acceptance of controls for the system. In Figure 11.1 this would represent control sets 1, 2, 3, and so on until the ROI bottoms or becomes zero. This is the break-even point, represented in Figure 11.1 as the intersection of the cost-of-controls curve and the expected-loss-due-to-exposure (after controls) curve. In Table 11.2 this point occurs with the

TABLE 11.2   Cost-Effectiveness Table with Data

$ Exposure/Class Rank			Selected Control Set Decision							
Class Rank	Exposure Identification/Location	Risk	Ps	Ca	Cc	Net Cost	% ROI	Ce Rank	I	
1	2	3	4	5	6	7	8	9	10	
1	A4 at Control Point 1	29.9M	.8	23.9M	18.5M	5.4M	29	23	I	
2	C1 at Control Point 9	29.2M	1.0	29.2M	25M	4.2M	17	24		
3	C2 at Control Point 3	24M	.6	14.4M	800K	13.6M	1,700	4	I	
4	B2 at Control Point 6	18.2M	.9	16.4M	5M	11.4M	228	16	I	
5	A1 at Control Point 10	12.8M	1.0	12.8M	2M	10.8M	540	11		
6	B2 at Control Point 5	3.0M	.9	2.7M	500K	2.2M	440	13		
7	B2 at Control Point 4	2.4M	.8	1.9M	600K	1.3M	217	17		
8	A3 at Control Point 2	1.8M	.8	1.4M	1M	400K	40	21		
9	A3 at Control Point 1	1.4M	.5	700K	60K	640K	1,067	6	I	
10	A1 at Control Point 6	1.3M	.7	910K	100K	810K	810	9		
11	F1 at Control Point 2	900K	1.0	900K	1M	(100K)	(10)	26		
12	A4 at Control Point 9	396K	.6	238K	100K	138K	138	18		↑
13	A1 at Control Point 9	240K	.9	216K	20K	196K	980	7		
14	A2 at Control Point 6	240K	.8	192K	5K	187K	3,740	1		
15	B1 at Control Point 3	216K	.6	130K	5K	125K	2,500	2		
16	A4 at Control Point 8	200K	.7	140K	70K	70K	100	20		E
17	A1 at Control Point 1	60K	1.0	60K	6K	54K	900	8		X C
18	D1 at Control Point 1	25K	.9	22.5K	4K	18.5K	463	12		L U
19	A1 at Control Point 2	10K	.5	5K	200	4.8K	2,400	3		D E
20	A1 at Control Point 4	10K	.8	8K	1K	7K	700	10		D
21	A1 at Control Point 3	8K	.4	3.2K	200	3K	1,500	5		
22	A1 at Control Point 8	2K	.9	1.8K	800	1K	125	9		
23	B1 at Control Point 11	200	1.0	200	50	175	350	14		
24	A1 at Control Point 7	20	1.0	20	5	15	300	15		
25	A1 at Control Point 5	2.5	.8	2	2	0	0	25		
26	A1 at Control Point 11	2.0	1.0	2	1.5	.5	33	22		↓

class rank exposure number 25. This arrangement of controls, however, is not necessarily the most effective. The problem with this ranking is that some of the greatest exposure risks are considered last; for example, class-ranked exposure number one, A4 at Control Point 1, is ranked 23rd by ROI. If management requires a minimum ROI for acceptance, many of the greatest risks still prevail. Even when the dollar return is met, the system may still be inadequately controlled (Ce rank 4). Furthermore, outside agencies such as the IRS may mandate control over an exposure *regardless* of ROI.

ADEQUACY OF CONTROLS

The adequacy of controls may be best determined by measurement to a predetermined acceptable level of dollar risk. For example, if management and audit of a $1.5 billion organization agree that any exposure with a cost/loss less than $500,000 is an acceptable level of risk, then the adequacy of controls depends on controlling each exposure to a maximum cost/loss value of $500,000.

If this criterion is applied to Table 11.2, Column 10 indicates those exposures that are inadequately controlled (I). The designer or auditor can now focus attention on those particular exposures and controls for reconsideration. The available options may be:

1. A complete redesign of controls
2. A revised estimate of risk
3. Reduction in the cost of the controls
4. Increase in the probability of control success
5. Acceptance; plus an additional set of controls for the remaining risk, and so on, until the remaining risk is under $500,000.

For example, the number one class-ranked exposure, A4 at Control Point 1, still has $6 million of risk remaining after applying the initial control set. This exposure, therefore, is inadequately controlled. The designer has any of the five options available to reduce this risk to $500,000 or less. Therefore, using an established management acceptability of risk value as a criterion for control design, Column 10 provides a listing of adequate control considerations for both the designer and auditor. This is a very helpful and effective tool.

In Table 11.2, class-ranked exposures 12 through 26 have no need for inclusion even though the ROIs on some are extremely great (for ex-

ample, 2400% for exposure 19). The focus is on spending company resource dollars on controls for exposure cost/loss risks greater than
$500,000.

Although an exposure may be adequately controlled, it still needs
to be cost-effective. For example, class-ranked exposure 11, F1 at Control Point 2, is adequately controlled; however, the cost of the control is
greater than the avoided risk. Such exposures also need reconsideration
by one or more of the available options.

FINAL SELECTION

Final consideration is now directed at exposures class-ranked 1 through
11 in Table 11.2. Common sense and reasonableness are applied. For
example, class-ranked exposure 11 is obviously in need of redesign before consideration of inclusion. The low ROI of class-ranked 2 (17%),
even though adequately controlled, makes it a candidate for restudy.
Then, the remaining inadequately controlled exposures 3, 4, and 9 need
review. A final recommendation can then be made. Table 11.3 illustrates
such revisions for recommendation.

The final selection of controls presented in Table 11.3 was influ-
enced by two major objectives: (1) the management risk objective of
limitation to $500,000 or less for any given exposure, and (2) an ROI of
40% or greater. Thus both considerations determined the final selection.

A decision was made for the first class-ranked exposure, A4 at
Control Point 1, to add additional control sets. This approach was
prompted by the designer's inability to revise the original control set for
any improved performance in cost and ROI. Since the net ROI after applying the first set of controls (29%) is well below the targeted 40%, the
additional sets must have substantially higher ROIs to pull the total
combined cost/control performance to 40% or better.

Note.   The additional two control sets to the original set of controls are considered to be independent events rather than mutually ex-
clusive events. In other words, no interdependency is assumed among
control sets. If any objection is made, the practitioner should consider
them as one lump control set rather than being dragged into a tremendous loss in time and dollars to debate the statistical permutations and
combinations. Only "God" knows the *exact* identification and interdependency of such controls.

The second set of controls selected for addition displays the following effect:

TABLE 11.3 Cost-Effectiveness—Final Selection

	$ Exposure/Class Rank		Selected Control Set Decision							
Class Rank	Exposure Identification/Location	Risk	Ps	Ca	Cc	Net Cost	% ROI	Net ROI	Net Risk
1	2	3	4	5	6	7	8		
☞ 1	A4 at Control Point 1	29.9M	.8	23.9M	18.5M	5.4M	29	29	6M
	Same (additional set)	6M	.9	5.4M	2.0M	3.4M	170	43	600K
	Same (additional set)	600K	.5	300K	50K	250K	500		
	(CONTROL PACKAGE)	29.9M	.99	29.6M	20.55M	11.05M	50.6	54	300K
☞ 2	C1 at Control Point 9	29.2M	1.0	29.2M	20M	9.2M	46	46	0
☞ 3	C2 at Control Point 3	24M	.8	19.2M	2.0M	17.2M	860	860	4.8M
	Same (additional set)	4.8M	.9	4.3M	4.0M	300K	7.5	292	500K
☞ 4	B2 at Control Point 6	18.2M	1.0	18.2M	12.2M	6M	49	49	0
5	A1 at Control Point 10	12.8M	1.0	12.8M	2M	10.8M	540	540	0
6	B2 at Control Point 5	3.0M	.9	2.7M	500K	2.2M	440	440	300K
7	B2 at Control Point 4	2.4M	.8	1.9M	600K	1.3M	217	217	500K
8	A3 at Control Point 2	1.8M	.8	1.4M	1M	400K	40	40	400K
☞ 9	A3 at Control Point 1	1.4M	.9	1.26M	650K	610K	94	94	140K
10	A1 at Control Point 6	1.3M	.7	910K	100K	810K	810	810	120K
☞ 11	F1 at Control Point 2	900K	.6	540K	300K	240K	80	80	360K

1. Risk is reduced to $600,000 ($6M–$5.4M).
2. ROI of this set is 170%.
3. Combined net ROI is 43%.

The third set of controls selected for addition displays the following effect:

1. Risk is reduced to $300,000.
2. ROI of this set is 500%.
3. Combined net ROI is 54%.
4. The target risk minimum ($500,000 or less) is reached.
5. The target ROI minimum (40%) is achieved.

The line labeled "Control Package" in Table 11.3 summarizes the evaluation. The Ps of .99 was derived in the following manner:

1. After applying control set 1, a Ps of 20% was lacking.
2. The second set of controls added was 90% successful over the remaining 20%, or 18% effective.
3. The third set of controls selected for addition was 50% successful over the remaining 2% risk, or 1% effective. Therefore, the final Ps for the package was estimated at 99%. Once again, this implies *independent* events. Although this may not be truly realistic, it is sufficient in achieving the objective at this point: a plausible set of controls for recommendation.

Exposure F1 at Control Point 2, although adequately controlled, presented an unacceptable ROI of minus 10%. Table 11.3 shows that a completely different set of controls was designed with lower cost and a lower Ps that met both design objectives.

Final review of Table 11.3 reveals that all exposures that warranted attention were redesigned to conform to management's basic objectives of ROI and risk.

REQUIREMENTS

Notice that the study effort is greatly reduced by using an acceptable level of risk value as a measure of adequacy of control. The total effort required to achieve these results is also minimized by *having a computer prepare all the forms, calculations, and outputs*. The practitioner need be concerned only with the input data and analysis. Therefore, a four- to six-week study period is generally quite adequate to accomplish this task.

SUMMARY

Table 11.1 is an extremely powerful tool for summarizing the data security risk analysis study of the system. It permits a concentration of work effort on only those items needing consideration. The use of a computer to perform the calculations and displays is definitely recommended for repetitive studies. The use of an acceptable level of risk agreed on by management and audit provides a method for assessing the adequacy of controls. In small companies ($1–2 million) this value may be as low as $25,000, whereas in very large organizations ($1–2 billion) a value of $500,000, such as used in Table 11.2's analysis, is very possible.

Final recommendations for system controls are now based on cost-effectiveness and acceptable level of risk. These measurements are familiar terms to, and generally accepted by, management.

12

"QUIK" APPROACH

The methodology presented in Chapters 5 through 11 for identifying exposures, focusing on control points, mapping exposures to control points, assessing risk, selecting controls, and applying a cost-effective controls decision may be abbreviated, if desired, for purposes of a quick ("Quik") analysis. This approach is presented as an alternative to designers and auditors who are interested only in a quick, first-blush overview of the state of the system. It provides a general system assessment rating and also points out potential areas for further control consideration. It does not replace the methodology presented for performing a detailed study.

Chapters 5, 6, 9, and 10 are summarized on a single workpaper as illustrated in Figure 12.1. The form presented in Figure 12.1 uses all the basic concepts previously presented—namely:

1. The six basic data exposures, Step 2. (Accidental/intentional; disclosure, modification, destruction.)
2. The six major causes of exposure, Step 3. (People, hardware, software, communications, acts of God, procedures.)
3. The three major types of controls, Step 4. (Preventive, detective, corrective.)

To use this form effectively, the following five-step approach illustrated in Figure 12.1 is recommended:

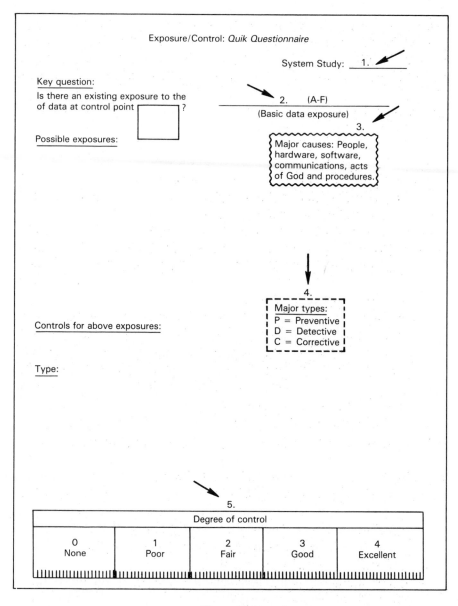

Exposure/Control: *Quik Questionnaire*

System Study: ___1.___

Key question:

Is there an existing exposure to the
of data at control point [ ] ?

2.   (A-F)
(Basic data exposure)

3.

Major causes: People,
hardware, software,
communications, acts
of God and procedures.

Possible exposures:

4.

Major types:
P = Preventive
D = Detective
C = Corrective

Controls for above exposures:

Type:

5.

Degree of control				
0 None	1 Poor	2 Fair	3 Good	4 Excellent

Figure 12.1

1. For purposes of later identification, the name of the particular system study is stated at the top of each form. If desired, the date on which this form is completed is also included.

2. Six worksheets, one for each of the six basic data exposures, are used for each control point considered. They are pictured in Figure 12.2 as worksheets A–F. Therefore, if the study flowed through all

Quik Questionnaire Control Point Set

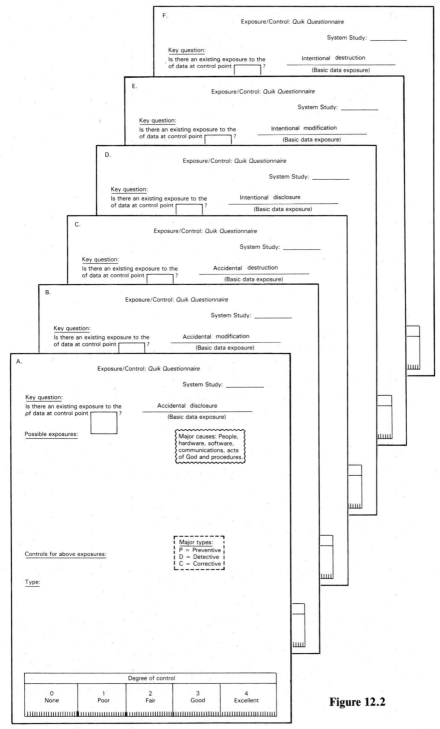

Figure 12.2

eleven control points and exhibited all six basic exposures at each point, a grand total of 66 worksheets would be generated. This would provide complete documentation of the system study. Most studies may call for only half that amount of documentation. In fact, if the focus of a "Quik" study is centered on only one specific control point, say Data Receipt, less than six sheets may be required.

3. For each positive answer to the "Key Question," the possible exposures are identified, defined, and documented. A comprehensive list is obtained by thinking through the six major causes of each basic exposure for the system at that particular control point.

4. Each defined exposure is reviewed for control considerations. These are viewed as possible sets of controls made up of the three major types (see Chapter 10). Whatever type or types of controls seem most adequate and appropriate comprise the control set for that particular exposure. Some controls may effectively cover more than one exposure. Therefore, the total number of controls may be less than the total number of exposures.

   The controls for the exposures listed on the "Quik Questionnaire" are used by the designer for documenting the control measures considered for inclusion in the system. They are used by the auditor for reviewing and assessing the adequacy and effectiveness of the control as well as compliance with established policy and procedure.

5. The assessment of risk on this worksheet provides for a subjective evaluation by the person or persons *responsible* for data at this control point as to the overall degree of control represented. The appropriate box is marked and initialed by the responsible party. If desired, a comment on the assignment of this value may be stated above the rating box.

"QUIK QUESTIONNAIRE" USAGE

The use of the "Quik Questionnaire" may be illustrated by reference to the previously mentioned payroll application example (Chapter 7). Figure 12.3 now shows a completed form for all the type "B" data exposures (accidental modification) at Control Point 1. For example, five possible exposures for accidentally modifying payroll are defined. The controls described are assessed as "Good" by the accountable payroll administrator assigned to that location.

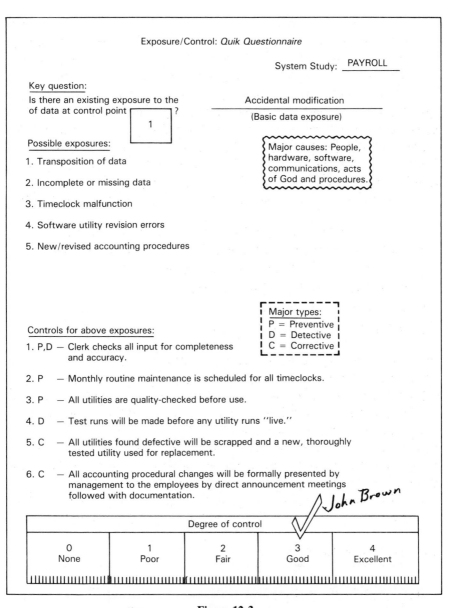

Figure 12.3

If this had been an audit review, the auditor would have judged the adequacy of control. Therefore, the controls listed in Figure 12.3 may be viewed either as those recommended by systems design or as those observed by audit. This form is excellent for capturing needed information from both such parties for a quick analysis. Most studies or reviews require no more depth of concentration than this form affords.

Upon completion of all questionnaires, the overall assessment of the entire system may be easily obtained by using the "Quik" General Assessment Matrix as shown in Figure 12.4.

The form presented in Figure 12.4 not only summarizes all the worksheets but also provides a visual picture of the control status. In order to demonstrate this benefit, Figure 12.5 is presented as a possible result from the payroll study example.

Note the following:

1. Each degree of control value is placed in its appropriate positional box. Hence, the "Good" or "3" rating assigned to the question of accidental disclosure at Control Point 1 is placed in the upper northwest block. Each cell, therefore, indicates individual control strength.

"Quik" General Assessment Matrix

Defined exposures		Control point ratings											
		1	2	3	4	5	6	7	8	9	10	11	Total
Accidental	Disclosure												
	Modification												
	Destruction												
Intentional	Disclosure												
	Modification												
	Destruction												
Total													

Grand total:

General assessment value:

Grand total ÷ 66 = _____

Figure 12.4

"Quik" General Assessment Matrix

Defined exposures		Control point ratings											
		1	2	3	4	5	6	7	8	9	10	11	Total
Accidental	Disclosure	3	4	3	4	0	2	4	3	4	3	3	33
	Modification	0	0	2	2	0	0	1	0	1	0	0	6
	Destruction	3	4	4	3	1	2	3	3	4	3	4	34
Intentional	Disclosure	4	3	3	4	0	2	3	4	3	4	3	33
	Modification	3	3	2	4	0	3	1	2	2	4	3	27
	Destruction	2	4	2	2	1	3	4	0	3	1	3	25
Total		15	18	16	19	2	12	16	12	17	15	16	
													158

Grand total:

General assessment value:

Grand total ÷ 66 = __2.39__ (fair)

Figure 12.5

2. A column indicates the total strength of control for a specific control point. Visually, Control Point 5 appears weak by observation of the numerous zeros. This may suggest a recommendation for a concerted control effort at these defined exposures.

3. A row indicates the total strength of control across all points for a specific type of defined exposure. Visually, accidental modification appears to be one of the greatest sources of control problems. This may suggest recommending a new control strategy for this type of exposure.

4. The grand total represents the overall general system assessment of data security. Figure 12.5's grand total of 158 translates into a 2.39, or a better than fair, rating.

The greatest improvement in overall system security can be easily gained by focusing on both the specific control points and particular data exposures that have very small values. Raising a zero to a 3 or 4 has far more impact than raising a 3 to a 4. For example, both Control Point 5 (total value 2) and accidental modification (total value 6) are ripe for improvement. If accidental modification were tightly controlled (4s across all control points), the overall system rank would increase to 2.97 or "Good." The matrix, therefore, provides a visual aid for spotting and selecting specific areas for improving overall system security.

The technique is simple, understandable, and effective to get a quick assessment in a relatively short time with minimum resources. Nevertheless, it has its shortcoming: it does not trade off the cost of the control to the cost of the exposure. Only an analysis as outlined in Chapter 11 provides this cost-effectiveness benefit.

The power of this approach lies in its capability to aid the practitioner in visually identifying and locating the weak links in the system's information security. Once the weak links are discovered, the practitioner may utilize any method for applying appropriate controls.

ABOUT THE APPENDIXES

The following contributed appendixes are to provide the reader with an example of how a corporate policy, assessment questionnaire, and other data security-related topics may be presented. The intent is to illustrate form, not to discuss the merits of content.

It is suggested that each organization develop its own particular plans, policies, programs, and questionnaires.

APPENDIX A

SECURITY ASSESSMENT QUESTIONNAIRE—IBM[1]

[1]Reproduced with permission IBM Corporation.

IBM

Security Assessment Questionnaire

This questionnaire has been prepared by the Data Processing Division of IBM to assist managers in making a self-assessment of their security position. While it is intended to be comprehensive, it is not exhaustive. For very sensitive environments, applications, or data, other tests may be indicated. It can be useful to DP management, general management, and auditors in evaluating and developing security programs and highlighting those areas that need additional management attention.

Instructions for Use

Questions are included to assess each of 14 categories in three key security areas:

- Physical Security
- Controls and Procedures
- Contingency Planning

Each question should be considered and a yes/no answer entered on the card. A "no" (or unknown) answer may be useful in identifying risks or identifying the need for protective measures. At the end of each category is an area to summarize your evaluation of the security position pertaining to that category. The following criteria may be useful in making that evaluation:

A. Extremely low risk (Opportunity to relax controls should be considered.)

B. Necessary risk only (No action indicated.)

C. Acceptable risk (This risk is known to and accepted by a level of management with sufficient discretion and resources for all corrective action.)

D. High risk (Action indicated.)

Also at the end of each category is one or more page-number references to documents cited in "Selected Publications" at the end of this questionnaire.

Physical Security

Fire	Yes	No
1. Is the building of modern fire-resistant construction or protected by fire-suppression systems?	—	—
2. Is the computer room isolated from combustibles (e.g., waste, forms, rags, tapes, office space, etc.) by two-hour rated fire walls?	—	—
From hazardous materials by four-hour rated walls?	—	—
Do the walls go from subfloor to super ceiling?	—	—
3. Is the computer room occupied three shifts a day or protected by automatic fire-suppression systems (e.g., sprinklers or HALON)?	—	—
Are spaces containing combustibles or hazardous material equipped with automatic fire-suppression systems appropriate to the material (e.g., water for paper)?	—	—
4. Is the computer room equipped with appropriate classes (i.e., A, B, C) of clearly visible fire extinguishers?	—	—
Are personnel trained and drilled in their use?	—	—
5. Are there sufficient fire and smoke alarms appropriate to the environment?	—	—
6. Are exits and evacuation routes clearly marked?	—	—
Are they equipped with emergency lighting?	—	—
7. Have provisions been made to detect and report fires on a timely basis?	—	—
8. Do fire hydrants, standpipes, ponds, or other sources provide sufficient water for fire-fighting?	—	—

2

Fire (cont'd.)   Yes   No

9. Are public or private fire departments located near enough to permit a timely response?   ——   ——

10. Has air-handling equipment been engineered so as not to fan the fire or spread heat, smoke or particulate matter (consider shut-offs, automatic dampers, etc.)?   ——   ——

11. Have all automatic fire-suppression systems been engineered (e.g., choice of suppressant, pre-alarms, manual overrides, etc.) to mini-mize hazards to personnel?   ——   ——

12. Have all unnecessary sources of ignition (e.g., smoking) been eliminated or identified and accepted?   ——   ——

    Is smoking prohibited in all areas containing combustible or flamma-ble material?   ——   ——

13. Are the DP facilities sited (near fire tower, at a level accessible to fire ladders, etc.) to permit ready access by fire fighting personnel and ready evacuation for DP personnel?   ——   ——

A	B	C	D

Reference: G520-2700-0
Pages 4—8

Rising Water   Yes   No

14. Is the computer room located on high ground or high in the building?   ——   ——

15. Are drains or other openings under the raised floor equipped with check valves?   ——   ——

16. Are water detectors and alarms used under the raised floor where necessary?   ——   ——

A	B	C	D

Reference: G520-2700-0
Pages 6—8

Falling Water   Yes   No

17. Is the ceiling free of plumbing and other water sources?   ——   ——

    Have cut-offs for any water in the ceiling been identified, are they accessible, and have they been labeled?   ——   ——

18. Is the ceiling free of any holes or defects that might permit water or any other substances to penetrate from above?   ——   ——

19. Has the use of water sprinkler systems been limited to those areas indicated by the type of construc-tion, presence of combustibles, and safety of personnel?   ——   ——

20. Have sprinkler systems over water-sensitive resources been engineered to minimize risk of water damage (e.g., recessed heads, on-off heads, dry-pipe systems, etc.)?   ——   ——

21. Has risk of falling water been compensated for by the availability of plastic sheeting?   ——   ——

Falling Water (cont'd.)   Yes   No

22. Have adequate provisions been
    made for the removal of water
    from computer room (e.g., drains,
    pumps, etc.)?   —   —

A	B	C	D

Reference: G520-2700-0
Pages 6—8

Intrusion   Yes   No

23. Are the computer room and other
    sensitive facilities (e.g., air-condi-
    tioning, mechanical, power distri-
    bution, air handling, communica-
    tions equipment, media and forms
    storage, etc.) located to be easily
    accessible only to authorized
    personnel (e.g., single occupancy
    building, inside control perimeters,
    high in the building, away from
    windows, away from public or
    high traffic areas, etc.)?   —   —

24. Are all windows to the computer
    room or other sensitive facilities
    inaccessible from the outside?   —   —

    Are accessible windows made of
    breakage-resistant material (e.g.,
    LEXAN)?   —   —

25. Is all access to such sensitive facili-
    ties via a single door (or limited
    number of doors) subject to direct
    observation by management or
    security personnel?   —   —

26. Are all control perimeters and
    approaches to sensitive facilities
    subject to observation either direct-
    ly or via closed circuit TV by
    management or security personnel?   —   —

Intrusion (cont'd.)   Yes   No

27. Are all emergency exit-only doors
    so labeled?   —   —

    Where such doors are not subject
    to management observation are
    they equipped with alarms?   —   —

28. Can access to the computer room
    and similar sensitive facilities be
    controlled by limited entrances,
    locks, badges, and observation, so
    that access is consistent with
    established policy? (See Controls
    and Procedures Question 34.)   —   —

29. Is the visibility of the computer
    room low (e.g., no signs, windows,
    or other unnecessary indicators of
    its presence)?   —   —

A	B	C	D

Reference: G520-2700-0
Pages 4, 5, 22

G320-5649-1
Page 20

Controls and Procedures

Organizational Controls

	Yes	No

1. Is the DP function separate from the using business function (e.g., accounts receivable, finance)? — —

   Does it report to a common level of management and enjoy a peer relationship with its users? — —

   Do all business transactions originate outside of DP? — —

2. At the level of the individual are data entry, operations, design and programming rigorously separated from each other and from use of the system? — —

   Are duties within each of these functions separated to a degree appropriate to scale of operation? — —

   Does this result in an acceptable level of business risk? — —

3. Is traditional segregation of function (e.g., transaction origination from approval, recordkeeping from custodianship, file maintenance from transaction processing, and transaction processing from procedure change) maintained in all application areas including program development? — —

4. Are duties assigned in such a manner that it is possible to fix accountability for all significant events and data to the level of a single individual? — —

5. Are procedures in place to inform all employees what resources they are expected to protect and from what hazards, what variances they are to note, and what corrective action they are to take? — —

Organization Controls (cont'd.)

	Yes	No

6. Has the responsibility for the protection of each and every resource been explicitly assigned? — —

   Is this assignment consistent with the right to say who may use the resource (ownership)? — —

7. In the normal course of events, is each person and each sensitive duty checked by another? — —

8. Is the number of people reporting to a single manager (i.e., span of control) consistent with the complexity and similarity of the function to be supervised (i.e., is the span narrower in systems programming than in data entry?) — —

   Is supervision sufficient to detect and correct errors? — —

9. Where indicated by the quantity, value, or sensitivity of resources, is there a security staff function? — —

A	B	C	D

Reference: G320-5649-1
Pages 7 & 8

G520-2700-0
Page 11

Personnel

	Yes	No

10. Are there hiring controls in place to ensure that all employees have the education and experience required for the job? — —

    Do these controls meet all policy, contractual, and legal requirements? — —

11. Is there a policy requiring mandatory vacations for all employees? — —

    Is it consistently enforced by line management? — —

7   8

Personnel (cont'd.)	Yes	No

12. Is there a practice of periodic job rotation for employees, first line managers, and supervisors? — —

13. Are special procedures in place to prevent misuse of employee accounts? — —

Are employees restricted from having accounts in ledgers they control? — —

Is all access to such accounts compensated for by additional management supervision? — —

14. Are procedures in place to ensure the timely and complete separation of terminated employees? — —

Are all authorities revoked and property reclaimed? — —

A	B	C	D

Reference: G320-5649-1
Pages 8 & 9

Operational Controls	Yes	No

15. Are procedures (e.g., proofreading, key verification, conversational feed-back, inspection, confirmations, etc.) in place to ensure the timely detection of errors? — —

16. Are controls (e.g., authorization, control totals, etc.) in place to enable using departments to ensure that all work was processed in accordance with their authorization and intent? — —

Are these controls reconciled on a regular basis? — —

17. Are controls in place to compensate for the sensitivity to error and misuse of error correction, recovery and restart, and IPL procedures? — —

Operational Controls (cont'd.)	Yes	No

18. Are there controls in place to fix accountability for all jobs submitted? — —

Are there procedures in place to ensure that output is delivered to the person for whom it is intended? — —

19. Are there controls (e.g., sequential numbers, separate custody) over sensitive input and output forms? — —

Are there controls (e.g., page numbers, last page indicators, etc.) to ensure the completeness of a printed report? — —

Are there controls to ensure that the proper number of copies are run and that all copies are accounted for? — —

20. Is there a policy consistent with generally accepted practice about who may access and update data? — —

Where indicated by the sensitivity of the resource and size of user population, is the policy enforced by the system? — —

A	B	C	D

Reference: G320-5649-1
Pages 9—11
G520-2700-0
Pages 13—17

IBM
®

International Business Machines Corporation
Data Processing Division
1133 Westchester Avenue, White Plains, N.Y. 10604

Printed in U.S.A. GX20-2381-0

Interface Controls	Yes	No

21. Is each individual user of the system uniquely identified? — —

22. Is there adequate evidence (e.g., password, magnetic-stripe card) to authenticate the identity of the individual user of the system? — —

23. Are users restricted to only those resources (e.g., data sets, records or segments, fields, transactions, etc.) required for their jobs? — —

24. Are the access rules up to date? — —

Are responsive procedures (e.g., security administration or online commands or transactions) for their update available to all responsible managers? — —

25. Are sufficient records kept to hold all users accountable for their use of the system and to fix account-ability for all changes to data and programs? — —

26. Are adequate mechanisms and pro-cedures in place to ensure that variances from the expected be-havior, use, or content of the system will come to the attention of responsible management in such a way as to permit timely and appropriate corrective action? — —

Will every variance be communicated to at least two people, including the owner of the resource and the manager of the user? — —

A	B	C	D

Reference: G320-5649-1
Pages 4—6

Application Development	Yes	No

27. Are there controls in place (e.g., phase reviews, inspections, walk-throughs, standards, independent acceptance, etc.) to ensure that programs do what and only what is intended? — —

28. Are there controls in place to ensure that resources allocated to program development are used only as intended? — —

29. Are there records adequate to fix accountability for all program changes to a specific programmer and authorizing and approving managers, with respect to both the fact of the change and its content? — —

30. Are all changes independently authorized and accepted by both development and user management? — —

31. Are programmers denied access to live systems, applications, data, and programs? — —

32. Are there standards in place for the use of appropriate high-level languages? — —

Are there standards in place that limit program scope (e.g., 50 lines or 50 verbs) and complexity (e.g., no crossing paths, limited number of total paths)? — —

Is there a requirement that all symbols come from a common, controlled source (e.g., dictionary or COPYLIB)? — —

33. Are programming controls at least as good as those employed for other applications (e.g., accounts receivable or payables)? — —

Application Development (cont'd.)

Yes No

Are they adequate to protect programmers and managers from unnecessary temptation and unwarranted suspicion?   — ——

A	B	C	D

Reference: G320-5649-1
Pages 11—16

Other

Yes No

34. Is access to sensitive facilities (or zones within them) limited to those people who work in that facility on that shift and authorized, escorted visitors?   — ——

    Is the number less than ten?   — —

35. Are authors or owners of data required to specify how it is to be protected?   — ——

    Are the specified measures appropriate to both the data and the media?   — ——

    Do these procedures avoid overprotection?   — ——

36. Are all employees and managers educated and trained in their security roles on a regular basis?   — —

37. Do all resources receive at least the minimum protection appropriate to sensitivity?   — —

    Are expensive measures reserved for sensitive resources?   — —

38. Is there regular independent review (e.g., by the audit or security staffs) of the application of these controls?   — ——

    Are variances reported to management?   — ——

    Corrective action taken?   — ——

A	B	C	D

Reference: G320-5649-1
Pages 7,8,11

13

Contingency Planning

General

Yes No

1. Does the DP department and its principal users have plans in place to deal with low frequency/high potential consequence events, such as storms, earthquakes, riots, bombs or the loss of essential services (e.g., power, heating/cooling, communications, transportation, etc.)?   — —

2. Are the plans documented in a manner adequate for the number of people who must know about them?   — ——

3. Has DP's plan been developed in conjunction with its users?   — —

    Are users informed that they still have the prime responsibility for their business functions in the event of the loss of the DP capability?   — —

    Is there agreement on working assumptions as to the frequency, severity, and duration of such outages, and to the backup and recovery strategies?   — —

4. Have the plans (user and DP) been reviewed and accepted by a common level of management?   — —

5. Have the plans been tested by drills, exercises, or third-party reviews?   — —

6. Have such tests been performed within the current year?   — —

7. At a minimum, do the plans provide that a current copy of all data essential to the continued operation of the business be stored off-site?   — —

8. Have all responsibilities under the plan been adequately documented and communicated?   — ——

A	B	C	D

Reference: G320-5649-1
Page 19

14

Emergency Yes No

9. Are provisions made to monitor all alarm sources including fire alarms, weather and emergency radio, etc.? — —

10. Has individual management responsibility for invoking contingency plans and for making decisions as to the necessary corrective action been clearly assigned? — —

   Have alternative individuals been identified? — —

11. Have provisions been made to notify all personnel what action (e.g., evacuation, shelter, etc.) they are to take? — —

12. Have employees been trained in emergency procedures (e.g., use of fire extinguishers, orderly shut-down, etc.)? — —

13. Are fire evacuation and shelter drills held on a regular and timely basis? — —

A	B	C	D

Reference: G320-5649-1
Page 17

Backup Yes No

14. Have all critical (non-discretionary) jobs (e.g., those related to cash-flow, such as billing; those related to product-flow, such as shipping and receiving; or those related to a billable service) been identified and prioritized? — —

15. Has the critical minimum configuration for all critical jobs been identified? — —

16. Have adequate alternative sources of processing capacity required for critical jobs been identified? — —

15

Backup (cont'd.) Yes No

17. Has a back-up supply of required forms been provided for? — —

18. Has the ability to run the critical jobs in the identified capacity been demonstrated? — —

19. Have decision criteria (e.g., will clearly be unable to resume processing at normal site within 24 hours) and authority for invoking back-up plans been identified? — —

A	B	C	D

Reference: G320-5649-1
Pages 17, 18

Recovery

20. Have all resources (e.g., people, plant communications, DP equipment, supplies, data, etc.) necessary to permanent recovery been identified? — —

21. Have sufficient alternative vendors or sources of supply for each of these resources been identified so as to result in an acceptable level of risk? — —

A	B	C	D

Reference: G320-5649-1
Pages 18, 19

16

Selected Publications

IBM Publications

Considerations of Physical Security in a Computer Environment (G520-2700)

Data Security Controls and Procedures (G320-5649)

Management Controls for Data Processing (GF20-0006)

Systems Auditability and Control, Audit Practices (G320-5790)

Systems Auditability and Control, Executive Report (G320-5791)

Systems Auditability and Control, Control Practices (G320-5792)

Other Publications

Computer Audit Guidelines
Canadian Institute of Chartered Accountants
250 Bloor Street East
Toronto, Canada M4W1G5, 1975
This document can also be obtained from
Institute of Internal Auditors
550 Diplomat Circle
Orlando, FL 32810

Computer Control Guidelines
Canadian Institute of Chartered Accountants
250 Bloor Street East
Toronto, Canada M4W1G5, 1970
This document can also be obtained from
Institute of Internal Auditors
550 Diplomat Circle
Orlando, FL 32810

Guidelines for ADP Physical Security and Risk Management, FIPS PUB 31, SD Catalog No. C13.52:31
National Bureau of Standards Publications
Superintendent of Documents
U.S. Government Printing Office
Washington, DC 20402, June 1974

Other Publications (cont'd.)

Protection of Electronic Computer/Data Processing Equipment, NFPA Standard No. 75
National Fire Protection Association
60 Batterymarch Street
Boston, MA 02110

17   18

APPENDIX B

GUIDELINES FOR DP ASSET PROTECTION—IBM[1]

SUBJECT: DATA PROCESSING ASSET PROTECTION

Concept

DP asset protection is selective application, in data processing environments, of protective measures supplemental to normal business controls, safety practices, and general provisions for physical security. While errors, accidents and omissions constitute the major hazards in a DP environment, the focus of this document is on protection from intentional acts and their consequences. Appropriate business controls are assumed to be in effect to deal with accidental events. The recommendations in this document may not be effective in the absence of such normal business controls.

The objectives of DP asset protection are to provide an additional level of protection including to:

- Prevent misuse and loss of DP assets; and
- Establish and preserve management options and legal remedies, in event of asset loss or misuse.

[1]Reproduced with permission IBM Corporation.

These Guidelines interpret basic asset protection requirements for application in data processing environments and establish additional requirements, as needed.

Purpose of Guidelines

- To establish *responsibilities* for protection of data processing assets.
- To establish the requirement for proper *business controls* in all data processing applications.
- To establish *minimum requirements* for DP asset protection.
- To establish the *basis* for DP asset protection *audits and self-assessments*.

Scope

These Guidelines apply to all "suppliers" and "users" of data processing services, and to all "owners" and "custodians" of data processing assets. These terms will be thoroughly defined, as they are basic to an effective asset protection program.

Covered are central processing, remote computing, distributed processing, shared logic processing, electronic correspondence, text processing, office systems, word processing, and digital transmission including product and field support.

CONTENTS

L. Glossary

M. Index

Note. The glossary must be consulted for full understanding of these guidelines!

A. STAFF RESPONSIBILITY

A1. Scope

This section describes the staff overview responsibilities of the Corporate Director of Security and the Corporate Director of Information Systems, and of the senior Security and Information Systems executives of the organizational units, with respect to DP asset protection.

A2. Corporate Director of Security Staff Responsibility

The Director of Security is responsible for general security throughout the Corporation, and will:

Establish overall security objectives and goals for the Corporation.

Develop Corporate security practices, instructions, and guidelines, and recommend policies for security.

Review proposed data processing asset protection practices, standards, instructions, and guidelines.

Provide direction, advice, and counsel to security organizations, users of data processing services, and owners of data processing assets.

Review the security component of business operating (1-2 years) and strategic (3 + years) plans and resolve open security issues.

Act as the Corporate security focal point for all organizational units on matters of overall security.

Conduct investigation of DP asset protection related security incidents as appropriate.

Develop, evaluate, and recommend DP systems when used principally for a security application.

Ensure that security staff, users of DP services, and owners of DP assets are provided effective education and direction with respect to DP asset protection responsibilities and requirements.

Develop methods and techniques to evaluate the effectiveness of security systems.

Monitor overall DP asset protection compliance throughout the Corporation.

A3. Corporate Director of Information Systems Staff Responsibility

The Director of Information Systems has DP *asset protection* responsibility for all internal data processing throughout the Corporation, and will:

Serve as the Corporate focal point on matters of DP asset protection.

Recommend Corporate DP asset protection policies, and establish DP asset protection objectives and goals for the Corporation, in support of overall Corporate security policies, objectives, and directives.

Develop, publish, and interpret Corporate DP asset protection practices, directives and guidelines, in support of Corporate general security policies, objectives, and directives.

Review security-related Corporate practices, directives, and guidelines.

Provide direction to the organizational units, with respect to DP asset protection.

Consult with the organizational units regarding placement of key Information Systems personnel having DP asset protection responsibility in the organizational units.

Ensure that suppliers of DP services are provided effective education and direction, with respect to DP asset protection responsibilities and requirements.

Monitor compliance of suppliers of DP services, and of data processing applications, with respect to DP asset protection.

Review the DP asset protection components of strategic and operating plans, and monitor performance of plan commitments with respect to suppliers of DP services.

Provide for assistance, as appropriate, in investigations and in education of users, owners, and security staff.

Initiate internal efforts, when necessary and feasible, to develop DP asset protection capabilities.

Provide for review and consultation with respect to software and hardware products offering asset protection capability.

A4. Organizational Unit Security Staff Responsibility

The senior Security executive is responsible for general security throughout the organizational unit, and will:

Establish overall security objectives and goals for the organizational unit, consistent with the Corporation's overall security objectives and goals.

Develop or initiate organizational unit security practices, instructions, and guidelines based on Corporate instructions and company policies.

Review proposed organizational unit implementation of DP asset protection standards, instructions, and guidelines.

Provide direction, advice, and counsel to location security organizations, users of DP services, and owners of DP assets.

Ensure appropriate security coverage in the operating unit's operating plans and strategic plans.

Act as the organizational unit security focal point for all locations on matters of overall security.

Conduct investigation of DP asset protection related security incidents as appropriate.

Recommend DP systems that could be used principally for a security application.

Ensure that security staff, users of DP services, and owners of DP assets are provided effective education and direction with respect to DP asset protection responsibilities and requirements.

Evaluate the effectiveness of security systems used in the locations.

Monitor overall DP asset protection compliance in the organizational unit.

Encourage ongoing liaison on DP asset protection matters among suppliers and users of DP services, owners and custodians of DP assets, the records management function, and the security function.

A5. Organizational Unit Information Systems Staff Responsibility

The senior information systems executive has DP *asset protection* responsibility for all internal data processing throughout the organizational unit, and will:

Serve as the organizational unit focal point on matters of DP asset protection, including interpretation of DP asset protection requirements, communication with Corporate Information Systems, and communication with suppliers of data processing services within the organizational unit.

Establish DP asset protection objectives and goals for the organizational unit, in support of Corporate and organizational unit security and DP asset protection policies, objectives, and directives.

Develop and publish organizational unit DP asset protection practices, directives, and guidelines, in support of Corporate and organizational unit security and DP asset protection policies, objectives, and directives.

Review security-related organizational unit practices, directives, and guidelines.

Consult with the business locations regarding placement of key Information Systems personnel having DP asset protection responsibility in the locations.

Ensure that suppliers of DP services are provided effective education and direction with respect to DP asset protection responsibilities and requirements.

Ensure that suppliers are effectively supported in development of DP asset protection plans and programs.

Coordinate DP asset protection self-assessment activity, and prepare the DP asset protection components of the organizational unit's strategic and operating plans.

Provide for assistance, as appropriate, in investigations, and in education of users, owners, and security staff.

Monitor suppliers' DP asset protection self-assessments, and their compliance with DP asset protection requirements.

Monitor application reviews and off-premises terminal programs.

Monitor suppliers' performance of DP asset protection commitments in strategic plans, operating plans, DP asset protection plans, and audit responses.

Initiate internal efforts, when necessary and feasible, to develop DP asset protection capabilities.

Encourage ongoing liaison on DP asset protection matters among suppliers and users of data processing services, owners and custodians of data processing assets, the records management function, and the security function.

The organizational unit's senior Information Systems executive will *ensure that a* DP *asset protection manager or program manager is assigned in his organization to assist in fulfillment of these responsibilities.*

B. USER, OWNER, CUSTODIAN, AND MANAGEMENT RESPONSIBILITY

B1. Mandatory Compliance

Fulfillment of DP asset protection responsibilities must be mandatory, and should be considered a condition of continued employment.

B2. User Responsibility

Users of data processing services and facilities are responsible for:

Using the company's data processing assets only for proper business purposes;

Effective use of control facilities and capabilities;

Performance of applicable ownership and custodian duties;

Compliance with applicable DP asset protection practices and directives, and with owner-established business controls and asset protection requirements; and

Initiating risk acceptance procedures, when compliance with required DP asset protection controls will cause an unacceptable business impact—see par. C2.

B3. Owner Responsibility

The terms "owner" and "ownership," with respect to assets, refer to responsibilities delegated to an identified employee or agent.

Ownership conveys authority and responsibility to:

Judge the asset's value and importance;

Specify business controls;

Classify the asset and specify asset protection controls, using a Selective Protection of Assets approach;

Authorize access and assign custody;

Communicate control and protection requirements to custodians and users;

Monitor compliance; and periodically review control and classification decisions.

The owner's responsibility to monitor compliance must not be construed as replacing the Security and I/S staff overview function, or as diluting custodian and user responsibility for compliance with DP asset protection requirements.

The owner is not directly accountable for a custodian's or user's noncompliance. However, the owner is expected to take reasonable steps to understand conditions surrounding the custody or use of the asset, to initiate appropriate actions when problems are identified, and to participate in custodian and user risk acceptance decisions.

The owner's responsibility to monitor may be delegated, but only if such delegation is supported by a documented agreement clearly stating the delegated commitments and responsibilities.

B4. Custodian Responsibility

Custodian responsibility includes the obligation to exercise sound business judgment, to comply with applicable directives and agreements, and to administer owner-specified business and asset protection controls.

Custodians may accept delegation of authority to grant access to classified information, but may not reclassify information.

Suppliers of DP services are typically custodians of application software and data, input received, and output produced by the data processing facility. As custodian, the supplier of DP services must administer, or provide for administration of, access to classified information, and provide physical and procedural safeguards.

When compliance with required controls cannot be achieved without causing an unacceptable business impact, the custodian must initiate the necessary risk acceptance procedures* as described in par. C2.

B5. Management Responsibility

With respect to DP asset protection, managers are responsible for:

Knowing assets for which they are responsible, and applicable control requirements;

Assignment of ownership authority and responsibility;

Assignment of custodian authority and responsibility;

Effective use of control facilities;

Employee education and awareness;

Timely, effective response to identified business control and asset protection exposures;

Timely, effective response to loss or misuse of assets; and self-assessment and planning.

B6. Self-Assessment and Planning

Self-assessments of DP asset protection status must be conducted at least annually, the end product being a committed DP asset protection plan, supported by a total accounting of compliance status.

In performing self-assessments, responsible management must:

Review asset protection responsibility assignments;

Review and validate classifications of software and data;

Identify exposures;

Validate risk acceptances; and

Develop documentation supporting the DP asset protection plan.

Diligent efforts must be made to identify all exposures. The status of each identified exposure must be shown to be that of *compliance with requirements, planned compliance, or risk acceptance.*

---

*In assigning custody of classified information, or delegating authority to grant access, the owner may require agreement by the custodian or delegate to perform duties related to such custody or authority.

C. COMPLIANCE

C1. Satisfactory Compliance

Mere installation of controls and procedures, while giving the appearance of compliance, may not produce required results. Satisfactory compliance is achieved when controls are effectively used.

Satisfactory compliance is characterized by:

Proper identification and classification of assets to be protected;

Consistency and continuity of control. In data processing applications, controls must be applied not only through software, but also procedurally and physically where people are involved—for example, in job submission, control of volumes, and release of output;

Effective prevention, so that collusion between two or more persons is required to avoid a control; timely detection and reporting of losses and improprieties;

Timely, effective response to reports of losses and improprieties; availability of information sufficient for after-the-fact investigation of loss or impropriety, and for appropriate management response, including personnel actions and pursuit of legal remedies; and

The attribute of auditability.

C2. Risk Acceptance

Responsible management may deviate from a control or protection requirement and accept an identified risk only when it has been clearly demonstrated that available options for achieving compliance have been identified and evaluated, and that compliance will have a significant and unacceptable business impact.

Risk acceptances must be documented, reviewed with affected parties, and noted in the DP asset protection plan.

Risk acceptances involving Confidential information, Sensitive Programs, control elements, or restricted utilities must be approved by local general management and communicated to appropriate organizational unit management.

Risk acceptances involving Registered Confidential information or information whose loss would be seriously damaging to the company must be approved by organizational unit general management, and *communicated to the appropriate Corporate Staffs.*

D. SOFTWARE AND DATA CONTROL

D1. Basic Classifications and Control
Statements

This paragraph summarizes controls established by classifications and control statements.

Classifications.   INTERNAL USE ONLY—only employees are allowed logical access and physical custody. Physical safekeeping and disposal must be in accordance with sound business judgment, so that the information will not be divulged outside the company.

CONFIDENTIAL—only authorized individuals are allowed logical access and physical custody. Must be kept under lock when not in use. Disposal method must assure destruction of the information content. (Requirements for disposal are modified for Confidential-Encrypted information—see par. E8 and H3, and Section F.) Single sealed enveloping or equivalent packing is required for internal mail and shipment; Certified Internal Mail or equivalent service is required for the internal transfer of Confidential information whose unauthorized disclosure would be seriously damaging to the company. Double sealed enveloping or equivalent packing is required for external mail and shipment. Encryption is required during electronic transmission of Confidential material whose unauthorized disclosure would be seriously damaging to the company.

REGISTERED CONFIDENTIAL—only authorized individuals are allowed logical access and physical custody. Must be stored separately from other material. Must be kept under adequate lock when not in use. Access, custody change, and disposal logs must be maintained by a Recorder. Disposal must be Recorder-controlled, and the disposal method must assure destruction of the information content. Reproduction must be Recorder-controlled. Recorder to Recorder transmission and physical transfer is required in all cases. Internal transfer must be via Certified Internal Mail or other service with equivalent control—single sealed enveloping or equivalent packing is required. External mail or shipment must be via U. S. Registered Mail—Return Receipt Requested, or U. S. Postal Express Mail, or equivalent service—double sealed enveloping or equivalent packing is required. Encryption is required during electronic transmission.

Control Statements.   DO NOT COPY—unauthorized reproduction is prohibited.

ENCRYPT FOR STORAGE—while encryption for online or offline storage is not required, this control statement may be used to indicate that such encryption is requested by the owner.

ENCRYPT FOR TRANSMISSION—to be used in conjunction with CONFIDENTIAL where encryption for transmission is required. (Not to be used in conjunction with the Registered Confidential classification, since all Registered Confidential transmissions must be encrypted, and the requirement is implicit in the Registered Confidential classification.)

FOR DEVELOPMENT USE ONLY—only individuals involved in research or product development activity may be allowed access.

SENSITIVE PROGRAM—see par. D6.

D2. Classifying Output

Output (including reports, data and software) containing substantially the same information content as the input must be assigned controls and classifications applicable to the input.

Output which is a substantial modification of the input information, or a merger of multiple inputs, must be classified and controlled on its own merits. See par. E2 regarding ownership of output.

D3. Classifying Software

Application programs developed for use within the company must be classified at least Internal Use Only.

Each form of software (source programs, object modules, procedures, etc.) must be separately classified and controlled on its own merits. For example, related source and load modules may be classified and controlled differently. See also par. E6, Logical access.

Applicable plain text classifications and control statements must be imbedded in all forms of the software (e.g., source, object, load, and dumps).

Associated documentation, punch card decks, mag cards, tapes, disks, cassettes, diskettes, etc., must carry external markings of applicable classifications. See par. E11 regarding computer output microfilm (COM).

D4. Classifying Volumes

A volume must be assigned the highest classification applicable to information it contains and, marked accordingly. The statement EN-CRYPTED must be applied when appropriate. See Section H. Control of Volumes.

D5. Classifying Dial Port Telephone Numbers

Telephone numbers of computer dial ports used for internal business must be classified at least Internal Use Only, and marked and controlled accordingly. These telephone numbers must not be published in telephone directories.

D6. Sensitive Programs

Application programs and associated procedures must be designated Sensitive Program and afforded the additional control described below, if fraudulent misuse resulting from unauthorized programming activity could result in serious misappropriation or loss of assets. "Associated procedures" include job control language used to invoke library update and link edit of application programs designated Sensitive Program.

Sensitive Programs will normally be associated with control, edit, or audit functions, or with creation of negotiable instruments. The following applications, among others, may contain software requiring Sensitive Program designation: Accounts Payable (including specialized applications such as Traffic); Accounts Receivable; Billing; Inventory control; Payroll (including related applications such as Personnel), bonds, stocks, taxes, and commissions; and Reimbursement Accounting (including Advances and Travel Expense Accounting).

Required Controls.   The purposes of Sensitive Program control are to prevent: unauthorized use, reproduction, modification or substitution of Sensitive Programs; unauthorized avoidance of controls; and unauthorized modification of control information.

Protective measures are required, in addition to normal installation and programming management, as follows:

Sensitive Programs, their owners, and custodians, must be identified and listed.

Written procedures must exist which describe the overall Sensitive Program control strategy, emergency procedures, and provisions for protection in backup and off-site storage situations.

Original specifications, and all changes, must be approved by responsible management, and kept in a controlled file.

Actual changes must also be kept in a controlled file. Timely, independent review must be conducted in advance of first production use, to assure that only authorized changes have been introduced into the production versions. Such reviews must be adequately documented and signed by responsible management.

Software modules and associated documentation must be internally marked:

SENSITIVE PROGRAM—UNAUTHORIZED
USE, MODIFICATION, OR REPRODUCTION IS PROHIBITED

Software must be access controlled, as appropriate, for read, update, and/or execution.

Access for update of production software must be approved by programming and installation management.

Programmers performing development or maintenance duties must not be cutodians of the production versions, nor be allowed access thereto.

Authorized persons may be allowed access only when doing authorized work.

Unauthorized reproduction must not be allowed.

Introduction and/or use of unauthorized copies or versions must not be allowed.

Reports—see par. E12.

D7. Control Elements and Restricted Utilities

Control Elements are software and data performing or supporting control functions such as access control, logging, and violation detection. Examples are: password data sets, files of cipher keys, log files, associated data reduction programs and hash total programs.

Restricted Utilities are software which can be used to alter or avoid control functions such as access control, logging, and violation detection.

Required Controls.   Control objectives are to prevent: unauthorized use, reproduction, modification, or substitution, of software control mechanisms; unauthorized avoidance of software controls; and unauthorized modification of control information.

Protective measures are required, in addition to normal installation and programming management, as follows:

> Control Elements and Restricted Utilities, their owners, and custodians, must be identified and listed.
>
> Written procedures must exist which describe the overall control strategy, emergency procedures, and provisions for protection in backup and off-site storage situations.
>
> Software must be access controlled, as appropriate, for read, update, and/or execution.
>
> Authorized persons may be allowed access only when doing authorized work.
>
> Access for update of production software must be approved by programming and installation management.
>
> Actual changes must be kept in a controlled file.
>
> Unauthorized reproduction must not be allowed.
>
> Introduction and/or use of unauthorized copies or versions must not be allowed.

Reports—see par. E12.

Displays or printouts of the information content of Control Elements and Restricted Utilities must be assigned the highest classification applicable to information contained or accessible, and controlled accordingly.

E. APPLICATION DESIGN AND REVIEW

E1. Design Review and Operational Review

This section provides asset protection guidance to owners, developers, custodians, and auditors of internal data processing applications under development, in operation, and undergoing enhancement or modification.

Internal applications under development or enhancement must be reviewed for compliance with these Guidelines, and approved before promotion to operational status.

Operational applications must be reviewed for compliance during self-assessment. See par. B6.

E2. Ownership

Owners of data processing applications, software, and data must be identified.

Data processing output (including reports, data, and software) is owned by the requesting user, unless other specific provisions are made.

Owners must:

Specify business controls;

Classify input, output, data, and software;

Designate Sensitive Programs, Control Elements, and Restricted Utilities;

Specify asset protection controls;

Approve business and asset protection controls as developed and implemented;

Monitor compliance with applicable controls, during development and enhancement, and when operational; and

Review classifications and controls for currency and adequacy at least annually.

See also par. B3, Ownership, and par. E3, Common applications.

E3. Common Applications

In addition to ownership responsibilities specified in par. E2, owners of common applications are responsible for the adequate documentation and communication of approved business and asset protection controls to all users and custodians of the common application, and for monitoring compliance at all using locations.

E4. Business Control

Appropriate business controls must be implemented in all data processing installations and applications. Business control of data processing services, software, and data includes: logon, transaction, and job submission control; input and output control; update control of data and software, including system control programs and libraries; detection of and recovery from errors, omissions, and aberrations; physical safekeeping; backup measures; and separation of duties.

E.5 Computer Access Control

Computer access, including terminal logon and job initiation, must be controlled on the basis of verified user identification and authorization. See par. E14, User and job identification, and E15, Verification passwords.

Installation management must assure that access authorizations are current, reflecting personnel and responsibility changes such as reassignments and separations. *Separations must be handled on an expedited basis.*

Provision must exist for nondisplay or blotting of classified passwords and identifiers.

Installation management must be able to change or deactivate any computer access authorization at any time. In addition, the user must be provided some means for deactivating his access authorization or changing his access code in event of known or suspected compromise.

Measures preventing repetitive attempts to gain unauthorized access must be in force.

E6. Update Control of Software and Data

Business control considerations require that update authority for software and data be controlled, and normally restricted to small populations of identified users. Similar restriction of read and/or execute authority may be required in some cases.

E7. Information and Transaction Access Control

Control of logical access to classified software and data, following logon or job initiation, must take into account all possibilities: read, update (including deletion), and execution.

Following logon or job initiation, logical access to classified transactions, software, and data must be controlled on the basis of previously validated user identification.

When access to information and transactions cannot be controlled in this manner, alternatives such as information access password protection or encryption must be used if available and practicable—see par. E16 and F4. Use of such alternatives will be on a risk acceptance basis—see par. C2, Risk acceptance.

Provision must exist for nondisplay or blotting of passwords and cipher keys.

Classified data and software must be associated with owner's identity, specified classifications and controls, and authorization lists as applicable.

Controls such as field within record, record within data base, and read-only and execute-only access, must be specified and implemented, when applicable.

Internal Use Only information must be appropriately protected against access by noncompany personnel.

In absence of an authorization list, only the owner may access software or data classified Registered Confidential or Confidential, or designated Sensitive Program.

Responsible management must assure that access authorizations are currrent, reflecting personnel and responsibility changes such as reassignments and separations. Separations must be handled on an expedited basis.

Information classified Registered Confidential or designated Encrypt for Transmission must not be accepted from or released to terminals deviating from requirements of par. I1 and I2.

E8. Disposal of Residual Information

Residual information in storage, volumes, and magnetic input/ output must be erased:

> Prior to decontrol of unencrypted Registered Confidential information and unencrypted Sensitive Programs; and of such information when encrypted, if requirements for generation and management of cipher keys are not met—see Section F.
>
> Prior to removal of the storage or volume from inventory control or from the restricted access area, or decontrol of the magnetic input/output, containing other unencrypted Confidential information, and encrypted Confidential information if requirements for generation and management of cipher keys are not met—see Section F.

Other classified, unencrypted residual information must be erased prior to disposal or noncompany use of the storage or magnetic input/ output.

Examples of erasure include degaussing tapes and mag cards, and overwriting disks, diskettes, mass storage cartridges, tapes, and main memory in nonvirtual systems.

Disposal of unencrypted Registered Confidential information must be reported twice-monthly to the Recorder.

E9. Software Testing

Information classified higher than Internal Use Only must not be used for software testing, except under specifically authorized and supervised conditions, such as final testing for newly developed or updated software.

E10. Input and Output

Classifications must:

Appear on the exterior of all input/output media such as card decks, mag cards, diskettes, cassettes, and volumes, See also Section H. Control of Volumes.

Appear on hard copy output separators and top sheets, so that they can be correctly handled while in installation custody.

Classifications, and control statements when applicable, must:

Be imbedded within information stored in output media. Use of header labels or volume table of contents for this purpose is satisfactory.

Be displayed on each page or frame of classified reports and other application output, including terminal displays and printouts.

Encryption must be performed as required. See par. D1 and J2. The original classification and control statements must be imbedded in, or otherwise associated with, the cipher text so that they will be known at time of decryption.

E11. Computer Output Micrographics (COM)

Classified COM output must be marked with applicable classifications and control statements which can be read without enlargement. In addition, each frame of classified COM output must contain applicable classifications and control statements.

At time of disposal, when destruction of information content must be assured, effective methods (e.g., burning or grinding) must be used. Shredding is not effective for this purpose.

E12. Access Activity Reports

Twice-monthly reports of access to Registered Confidential information (encrypted and unencrypted), and custody change activity, must be provided to Recorders.

Monthly reports of sensitive program activity must be provided to owners and installation management.

Recipients of these reports must analyze them and take timely action as indicated.

E13. Access Violations

Provision must be made for timely detection, reporting and analysis of unauthorized attempts to gain computer, software, and/or data access.

Responsibility for timely reaction to violations must be clearly assigned.

E14. User and Job Identification

User and job identification codes must be traceable to the user for the lifetime of the records and reports in which they appear.

E15. Verification Password Generation and Control

Installation and user management is responsible for assuring that passwords used to verify user or job identification are:

Of a length, and changed on a frequency, such that it is not possible to complete an exhaustive search before the password is changed;

Randomly selected and not obvious or trivial; and

Classified at least Confidential.

Minimum length, unless otherwise justified, must be the number of characters which yields at least 10^6 possible combinations—for example, at least 6 decimal digits, or 5 hexadecimal characters (16^5), or 5 alphabetic characters (26^5), or 4 alphanumeric characters (36^4).

Minimum change frequency, unless otherwise justified, must be every two months, more frequently when indicated by sound business judgment; and if user generated, not reused for at least fifteen months.

Users must prevent accidental and inadvertent disclosure of passwords.

E16. Information Access Password Generation and Control

Use of passwords for information access control following logon or job initiation is allowed only on a risk acceptance basis. See par. E7.

Information access passwords must not be obvious or trivial.

Information access passwords must be assigned the classification of the associated information, and controlled accordingly. All requirements for marking and communication of security classification are applicable.

Disclosure of information access passwords must be controlled so that all persons having the password are known to the owner or administrator. Registered Confidential password disclosure activity must be reported twice-monthly to the Recorder.

Users must prevent accidental and inadvertent disclosure of passwords.

Responsible management must assure that information access passwords are changed upon termination of the business need of any individual to whom the password has been disclosed, and at least every six months.

Passwords must be declassified following deletion or erasure of the protected information, and when they are no longer current.

See also par. F4, Control of cipher keys.

F. CRYPTOGRAPHY

F1. Use of Cryptography

Cryptography must not be used as a primary access control method, except on a risk acceptance basis as provided in par. E7. Cryptography may, however, be used as a supplemental measure to defeat unauthorized interception of information during electronic or physical transfer, and to defeat unauthorized access to information stored online or offline to a computer.

Cryptography's effectiveness for these purposes is directly related to the quality of cipher key generation and protection. In this respect, cryptography is comparable to data set and workspace password mechanisms, and presents analogous control problems. See par. E16.

F2. Precautions

WARNING. Compromise of cipher key means compromise of text. Loss of key means irretrievable loss of information unless clear text backup is kept.

Clear text backup should not be destroyed until the cipher key has been validated following encryption.

Storage of encrypted information entails retention of the cipher key and the correct version of cryptographic software or hardware, as well as the encrypted text.

F3. Cipher Key Generation

Input cipher keys must be 56 binary digits in length. When expressed in character sets other than binary, the length must be such that the number of characters yields at least 2^{56} possible combinations; for example, 17 decimal digits (10^{17}), 14 hexadecimal characters (16^{14}), 12 alphabetic characters (26^{12}), or 11 alphanumeric characters (36^{11}).

Keys must be randomly selected, and not selected for mnemonic value. See par. F5.

Caution must be exercised in the use of so-called random number algorithms for generating cipher keys. It must be determined that the output is sufficiently random for the purpose.

F4. Control of Cipher Keys

Cipher keys must be reduced to writing or some other form of record, assigned the classification applicable to the clear text, and controlled accordingly. All requirements for marking and communication of security classification are applicable.

When transferring encrypted information, keys must be communicated separately and securely.

Disposal of cipher keys must be accomplished by complete destruction or erasure.

Cipher keys must be declassified following erasure of the encrypted information.

Registered Confidential cipher key custody, disclosure, declassification, and disposal activity must be reported to the Recorder twice-monthly.

F5. Deviation

Deviations must be handled as risk acceptances—see par. C2—and information so encrypted must be controlled, decontrolled, and disposed of as though it were not encrypted.

G. COMPUTING INSTALLATIONS AND SUPPORTING FACILITIES

G1. Communication with Users and Owners

Suppliers of DP services must be fully informed of controls required for protection of assets in their custody.

Responsible management must effectively instruct application owners, information owners, and users on available control facilities, required and recommended practices, and installation restrictions.

Users must frequently and effectively be advised that services and resources are to be used for business purposes only.

G2. Restricted Physical Access

Computing installations and supporting facilities must be administered as areas of restricted physical access, if:

Continued operation is considered vital; or
Classified information is stored or processed in the installation.

Supporting telecommunication facilities such as telephone closets, wire rooms, and frame rooms must be administered as areas of restricted physical access.

Measures must be implemented to prevent and detect attempts to disrupt operations, or to enter or depart from restricted areas in an unauthorized or surreptitious manner. Responsibility must be clearly assigned for timely and effective response to such attempts.

Routine physical access (i.e., no escort or visual surveillance) must be allowed only to persons whose primary work stations are within the area at the time.

G3. Visitor Control

Each person in the installation must wear some readily visible indication of whether the person is a visitor, and whether the person is an employee.

All visitor entries and all nonroutine entries of regular installation personnel must be logged. Reports of visitor and nonroutine entry activity must be presented to installation management daily. Responsibility must be clearly assigned for timely followup.

In order to prevent unauthorized access to classified information, and to prevent unauthorized removal of classified information from the restricted access area:

> Authorized users and authorized support personnel must be kept under visual observation; and
>
> All other visitors must be escorted.

G4. Classified Materials

Classified input, output, software, and data must be protected, and released only to authorized recipients.

Controls must be in place for effective deterrence and timely detection of unauthorized attempts to access or remove classified information. Responsibility must be clearly assigned for timely and effective response to such unauthorized attempts.

Carbon paper, overrun copies, partial unusable output, etc., associated with classified information must be appropriately disposed of.

G5. Fire Protection

The computer area must be of noncombustible construction. Media and volumes in the computer area must be enclosed in fire-resistant cabinets or containers. Card and paper storage rooms must be of noncombustible construction and sprinkler protected.

H. CONTROL OF VOLUMES

H1. Logical Access Control

The mounting, demounting, and storage of all Mass Storage System cartridges, and of all classified volumes, must be administered to prevent unauthorized access to their information content.

H2. Inventory Control and Accountability

All volumes containing classified information (including residual classified information), must be inventory controlled. That is, every such volume must be uniquely identified and accounted for in an appropriate record keeping system. Accountability for the inventory must be clearly assigned.

It must be possible to fix specific personal responsibility for all volumes in the inventory containing unencrypted RC information, including such volumes in transit and in remote storage.

Volumes containing unencrypted Registered Confidential information must be inventoried weekly. All changes of physical custody must be reported twice-monthly to the Recorder.

Volumes containing unencrypted Confidential information must be inventoried at least every three months.

Other volumes containing classified information must be inventoried at least every six months.

H3. Safekeeping

All classified volumes must remain within the computing installation's restricted access except during authorized transfer to another installation's restricted access area and inventory control.

Authorization and control procedures must be in force with respect to removal of classified volumes from the installation.

Volumes containing unencrypted Registered Confidential information, or unencrypted information designated Sensitive Program, must be locked up when not actually in use, and when in use if not under continuous surveillance by the custodian.

Registered Confidential custody, declassification, and disposal activity, must be reported twice-monthly to the Recorder.

H4. Fire Protection

Storage rooms for master records and tapes must be of two-hour rated construction, and sprinkler protected.

I. TERMINALS

I1. Installation Management Responsibility

Suppliers of DP services are responsible for assuring that terminals accessing company computers, for the purpose of conducting internal company business, are under company control.

Registered Confidential information, and information designated Encrypt for Transmission, must not be accessible to terminals deviating from this requirement. See par. E7.

I2. Terminal User Responsibility

Terminal users are responsible for assuring that:

Terminals connected to Company computers or Company terminals for the purpose of conducting internal Company business, are under Company control. Registered Confidential information, and information designated Encrypt for Transmission, must not be received by or entered into terminals deviating from this requirement. See par. E7;

Dial terminals while connected, and permanently connected terminals while logged on, are attended by an authorized person;

Dial terminals while unattended, are disconnected from the computer or terminal, or disabled; and permanently connected terminals, while unattended, are disabled.

I3. Deviations

Terminals not under Company control when connected to Company computers or Company terminals must be managed in accordance with par. C2, Risk acceptance, observing the following specific requirements:

Business necessity must be certified by two levels of management;

Terminal must be operated in accordance with applicable safety, security, and DP asset protection requirements;

Provision must be made for protection of classified passwords and classified materials, and for disposal of classified waste;

Prior to final approval, the following functions must be notified and consulted, as appropriate: business controls, information systems, legal, personnel, safety and security; and

Approval must be for a specific period of time, not to exceed six months.

Requests for extension beyond the initial period of time may be approved only when found to satisfy all the above requirements.

J. MESSAGES AND TEXT

J1. Sending, Forwarding, and Receiving Stations

Company sending and receiving stations are responsible for marking messages and text with applicable classifications and control statements, and for proper handling.

Company sending, forwarding, and receiving stations are subject to requirements for Computing Installations and Supporting Facilities, Terminals, Volume Control, and Disposal of residual information. See Sections G, H, I, and par. E8.

J2. Messages and Text

Applicable classifications and control statements must be imbedded in transmitted messages and text.

Messages and text classified Registered Confidental, or designated Encrypt for Transmission, must be encryptetd during transmission.

Other Company Confidential messages and text may be transmitted unencrypted only if sending stations, receiving stations, and store and forward stations are under Company control. If not, encryption is required.

K. RECORDS

The characteristic of auditability is fundamental to all requirements established by these Guidelines. While "auditability" normally involves record keeping, management may select alternative methods of demonstrating compliance, except when specific record-keeping requirements are stated.

GLOSSARY

Asterisk (*) flags a term defined elsewhere in the glossary.

Access control.   Depending upon context, means control of a user's ability to use a data processing service, or control of logical access*.

Application. Means end use of data processing services and facilities. The scope of an application extends to: data processing services used or invoked, application programs and associated software, input, output, data, procedures, documentation, and responsibility assignments. Payroll and engineering design are examples of applications.

Asset protection. See *DP asset protection*.

Auditability. Is demonstrability. An auditable application is one whose performance according to specifications and compliance with business control and asset protection requirements can be demonstrated to, or formally tested by, an independent reviewer.

Business control. Is the management of a process or application. Business controls are functions and attributes which render the process or application manageable. Business controls enable management to safeguard assets and to prevent their loss or unintended use; to detect and understand errors, omissions, and aberrations; to take corrective actions; to verify correctness of results; and to recover from disruption. See par. E4.

Classified. For purposes of these Guidelines, means subject to prescribed asset protection controls, including controls associated with classifications and control statements.

Classify. For purposes of these Guidelines, means to specify asset protection controls and apply appropriate classification and/or control statements.

COM. Means computer output micrographics, including all computer-produced microforms such as rolls, fiche, aperture cards, etc.

Common application. Is information (software and/or data) developed for use within the company and distributed within the company.

Company control. (1) A terminal under Company control is either on company premises, or if not on Company premises, is nevertheless a Company employee's assigned work station for normal performance of duties. Terminals in employees' homes are not under Company control, for purposes of these Guidelines. (2) With respect to physical transfer of software or data, the information is under Company control if continually in custody of a Company employee, or of an agent specifically authorized by Company for this purpose. (3) With respect to messages and text, a sending, forwarding or receiving station is under Company control if it is managed, or specifically approved for this purpose by the Company.

Computer.   Is a central processor, distributed processor, shared logic processor, word processor, office system processor, digital transmission controller, etc.

Computing installation.   Is one or more computers*, together with attached memories and storage, used in the conduct of company business. Whether modified computers constitute a computing installation, or a terminal, or neither of these, depends on their use and is a matter of business judgment and risk acceptance. See *Supporting facilities* and *Terminal*.

Control element.   Is an application or system control program component (software or data) performing or supporting a control function such as access control, logging, or violation detection. Special control is required.

Cryptography.   Is the transformation of information from clear form into coded form (encryption) or from coded form into clear form (decryption). Digital cryptography manipulates input data (clear text or cipher text), together wth an input cipher key, to produce encrypted or decrypted output.

Custody, Custodian.   Custody is authorized possession of an asset. Custodian is an employee or agent having authorized possession. Custodians are responsible for business control and protection of assets in their custody. See par. B4.

Data.   Is processable information other than software*, together with the associated documentation.

Decontrol.   Is removal of access controls*.

Directive.   Means standard or instruction.

DP asset protection DPAP.   Is selective application, in data processing environments, of protective measures supplemental to normal business controls*, safety practices, and general provisions for physical security. The focus is on protection from intentional acts and their consequences.

DP assets.   Include computers*, computing installations*, terminals*, supporting facilities*, data processing services, and data processing input/output*, software*, and data*.

Information.   Includes input, output, software*, and data*.

Input/output.   Includes punched cards, magnetic input/output*, volumes*, and other forms of processable information used for computer input or produced as computer output, as well as reports, listings, COM*, and other forms of hard copy output.

Logical access.   Means access to the information content of a record.

Magnetic input/output.   Includes mag cards, cassettes, diskettes, and other mountable magnetic storage media not controlled as volumes*.

Messages.   Include transmissions, telegrams, cables, digital facsimile transmissions, electronic mail, point to point terminal and mag card operations, etc.

Monitor.   Means to be informed, and to initiate appropriate action when problems are identified.

Organizational unit.   As used in Section A, means operating unit, group, or Corporate Headquarters.

Owner.   Is an employee or agent assigned responsibility for making and communicating certain judgments and decisions regarding business control and selective protection of company assets, and for monitoring compliance with specified controls. See par. B3.

Recorder.   Is the Recorder of Registered Confidential* Records or an authorized Subrecorder.

Residual information.   Is readable information remaining from prior use of the storage*, volume*, or magnetic input/output*.

Restricted utility.   Is software which can be used to avoid controls or alter control information. Special control is required.

Review.   As used in Section A, implies the right of disapproval.

RC.   Means Registered Confidential.

Selective protection of assets.   Is selective application of protective measures to identified assets, supplemental to normal business controls, safety practices, and general physical security.

Sensitive program.   Is an application program whose misuse through unauthorized programming activity could result in serious misappropriation or loss of assets. Special control is required.

Software.   Is processable information in the form of computer programs, job control language, libraries of programs and procedures, microcode, microprocessor programs, etc. together with the associated documentation.

Storage.   Means a computer's nonmountable memory component, for example: main memory and drum storage.

Supporting facilities.   Are facilities supporting computing installations. Examples include: data entry areas; input/output areas; COM installations; bursting/decollating rooms; and power supply areas.

Terminal.   Means an input and/or output device located outside the computing installation's restricted access area, or within the area if user operated. Word processing stations, distributed processing stations, job entry stations, etc., can be terminals within this definition.

Visitor.   With respect to a computing installation restricted access area, is any person whose work station is not within the restricted area.

Volume.   Is a mountable storage device, such as a disk pack, mass storage system cartridge, or magnetic tape. In these Guidelines diskettes, cassettes, mag cards, etc., are treated as magnetic input/output*, but may optionally be controlled as volumes.

INDEX

APPENDIX C

DEFINITIONS OF APPLICATION CONTROLS[1]

[1]W. C. Mair, W. R. Wood, and K. W. Davis, *Computer Control & Audit*, 11A (1978), 98–105. Reprinted with permission.

APPLICATION CONTROLS: PREVENTIVE, DETECTIVE, CORRECTIVE

PREVENTIVE CONTROLS	EXPLANATION	EXAMPLE
Definition of Responsibilities	Descriptions of tasks for each job function within an information processing system. These indicate clear beginning and termination points for each job function. They also cover the relationship of job functions to each other.	The cashier disburses petty cash and prepares deposits but does not sign checks or maintain accounting records.
Reliability of Personnel	Personnel performing the processing can be relied upon to treat data in a consistent manner.	The cashier has a record for regular attendance, few errors, and keeping sober.
Training	Personnel are provided explicit instructions and tested for their understanding before being assigned new duties.	All tellers attend a one-week school before starting work.
Competence of Personnel	Persons assigned to processing or supervisory roles within information systems have the technical knowledge necessary to perform their functions.	The controller is a CPA.
Mechanization	Consistency is provided by mechanical or electronic processing.	Calculation of gross and net pay is performed by computer.
Segregation of Duties	Responsibility for custody and accountability for handling and processing of data are separated.	The cashier does not maintain the cash accounting records.
Rotation of Duties	Jobs assigned to people are rotated periodically at irregularly scheduled times, if possible, for key processing functions.	Payroll clerks are always rotated within two years.
Standardization	Uniform, structured, and consistent procedures are developed for all processing.	A controller's manual describes the processing of all financial applications.
Authorization	Limits the initiation of a transaction or performance of a process to the selected individuals.	Only the timekeeper may submit payroll-hours data.

Term	Description	Example
Secure Custody	Information assets are provided security similar to tangible assets such as cash, negotiable securities, etc.	The general ledger is locked in a safe every night.
Dual Access/Dual Control	Two independent, simultaneous actions or conditions are required before processing is permitted.	A safe deposit box requires two keys to open it.
Forms Design	Forms are self-explanatory, understandable, concise, and gather all necessary information with a minimum of effort.	The form to establish a new account has instructions for each space and spacing indicated to assist in keypunching.
Prenumbered Forms	Sequential numbers on individual forms printed in advance so as to allow subsequent detection of loss or misplacement.	Checks are provided with preprinted numbers.
Preprinted Forms	Fixed elements of information are entered on forms in advance and sometimes in a format which permits direct machine processing so as to prevent errors in entry of repetitive data.	The MICR encoding of bank and account number on checks.
Simultaneous Preparation	The one-time recording of a transaction for all further processing, using multiple copies, as appropriate, to prevent transcription errors.	A payment form having check, check copy, and voucher.
Turnaround Document	A computer-produced document which is intended for resubmission into the system.	A utility bill.
Drum Card	Automatic spacing and format shifting of data fields on a keypunch machine.	The tab key on a typewriter is replaced by a drum card on a keypunch.
Endorsement	The marking of a form or document so as to direct or restrict its further use in processing.	Endorsing a check "for deposit only."
Cancellation	Identifies transaction documents to prevent further or repeated use after they have performed their function.	Punching "PAID" into invoices.
Documentation	Written records for the purpose of providing communication.	Standard forms for journal entries.

PREVENTIVE CONTROLS	EXPLANATION	EXAMPLE
Exception Input	Internally initiated processing in a predefined manner unless specific input transactions are received that specify processing with different values or in a different manner.	A salaried employee must submit a separate request for payment of overtime.
Default Option	The automatic utilization of a predefined value in situations where input transactions have certain values left blank.	Salaried employees receive pay for a 40-hour week automatically.
Passwords	The authorization to allow access to data or processed by providing a signal or "password" known only to authorized individuals.	Computer access by a time-sharing terminal requires a user identification and a secret code word.

DETECTIVE CONTROLS	EXPLANATION	EXAMPLE
Anticipation	The expectation of a given transaction or event at a particular time.	Every employee expects his paycheck at 3 P.M., Friday.
Transmittal Document (Batch Control Ticket)	The medium for communicating control totals over movement of data, particularly from source to processing point or between processing points.	Receipts for deposit are accompanied by a deposit slip indicating the account, listing the currency and checks, and total.
Batch Serial Numbers (Batch Sequence)	Batches of transaction documents are numbered consecutively and accounted for.	Daily receipts are batched together and numbered, using the Julian date.
Control Register (Batch Control Log)	A log or register indicating the disposition and control values of batches or transactions.	A logbook records the time and batch number of receipts picked up by the armored-car service.
Amount Control Total	Totals of homogeneous amounts for a group of transactions or records, usually dollars or quantities.	The receivables file totals $1,237,629.53.
Document Control Total	A count of the number of individual documents.	The receivables file contains 3,721 accounts.

Term	Description	Example
Line Control Count	A count of the individual line items on one or more documents.	The December invoices had 4,261 line items.
Hash Total	A meaningless, but useful, total developed from the accumulated numerical amounts of nonmonetary information.	The hash total of account numbers is 47,632,177.
Batch Totals (Batch Control)	Any type of control total or count applied to a specific number of transaction documents or to the transaction documents that arrive within a specific period of time.	The December 17 invoices total $44,755.68.
Batch Balancing	A comparison of the items or documents actually processed against a predetermined control total.	A teller will compare currency and checks with the list and total on the deposit slip.
Visual Verification	The visual scanning of documents for general reasonableness and propriety.	A quick scan revealed that the printer's ink roll was dry.
Sequence Checking	A verification of the alphanumeric sequence of the "key" field in items to be processed.	Account number A16352 precedes account number A16567.
Overflow Checks	A limit check based upon the capacity of a memory or file area to accept data.	The product of $10,736 \times 37,667 =$ (404,392,912) cannot be displayed on an 8-digit calculator.
Format Check (Form)	Determination that data are entered in the proper mode—numeric or alphanumeric—within designated fields of information.	The characters 4 H 6 1 are not an acceptable invoice amount.
Completeness Check	A test that data entries are made in fields which cannot be processed in a blank state.	The computer will not print the check if the payee is all blanks.
Check Digit	One digit, usually the last, of an identifying field is a mathematical function of all of the other digits in the field. This value can be calculated from the other digits in the field and compared with the check digit to verify validity of the whole field.	(see calculation below)

```
                  5 6
     1   2   3   4   2
   × 2   1   2   1   2
  ───────────────────────
   2+  2+  6+  4+  10 = 24
                       2
                       1
                      10 = 24
                       - 30
                       ────
                         6
```

DETECTIVE CONTROLS	EXPLANATION	EXAMPLE
Reasonableness	Tests applied to various fields of data through comparison with other information available within the transaction or master records.	A male patient should not receive charges from the obstetrics ward.
Limit Check (Range Check)	Test of specified amount fields against stipulated high or low limits of acceptability. When both high and low values are used, the test may be called a "range check."	A paycheck should be between zero and $900.
Validity Check	The characters in a coded field are either matched to an acceptable set of values in a table or examined for a defined pattern of format, legitimate subcodes, or character values, using logic and arithmetic rather than tables.	375-44-006 is not a proper social security number. They all have nine digits.
Read Back	Immediate return of input information to the sender for comparison and approval.	Information transmitted over the phone is repeated back to the sender.
Dating	The recording of calendar dates for purposes of later comparison or expiration testing.	A date is placed on all paychecks.
Expiration	A limit check based on a comparison of current date with the date recorded on a transaction, record, or file.	The paycheck is marked "void after 90 days."
Keystroke Verification	The redundant entry of data into keyboards so as to verify the accuracy of a prior entry. Differences between the data previously recorded and the data entered in verification will cause a mechanical signal.	A punch card verifier closely resembles a keypunch.
Approval	The acceptance of a transaction for processing after it has been initiated.	The controller approves the journal entry prepared by the payroll clerk.

Term	Description	Example
Run-to-Run Totals	The utilization of output control totals resulting from one process as input control totals over subsequent processing. The control totals are used as links in a chain to tie one process to another in a sequence of processes or one cycle to another over a period of time.	Beginning receivables plus invoices and minus receipts and adjustments should equal the ending receivables balance.
Balancing	A test for equality between the values of two equivalent sets of items or one set of items and a control total. Any difference indicates an error.	The detail of accounts receivable differs from the general ledger by $326.11.
Reconciliation	An identification and analysis of differences between the values contained in two substantially identical files or between a detail file and a control total. Errors are identified according to the nature of the reconciling items rather than the existence of a difference between the balances.	The bank reconciliation indicates an unrecorded service charge as well as outstanding checks and deposits in transit.
Aging	Identification of unprocessed or retained items in files according to their date, usually transaction date. The aging classifies items according to various ranges of dates.	Receivables are aged "current, 30, 60, 90, over 90."
Suspense File	A file containing unprocessed or partially processed items awaiting further action.	The receivables file contains invoices on which neither payment nor partial payment was received.
Suspense Account	A control total for items awaiting further processing.	The total value of the receivables file should agree with the general ledger balance for receivables.
Matching	Matching of items from the processing stream of an application with others developed independently so as to identify items unprocessed through either of the parallel systems.	The payables clerk matches purchase orders to receiving reports and invoices.

DETECTIVE CONTROLS	EXPLANATION	EXAMPLE
Clearing Account	An amount which results from the processing of independent items of equivalent value. Net control value should equal zero.	Intercompany accounts should eliminate upon consolidation.
Tickler File	A control file consisting of items sequenced by age for follow-up purposes. Such files are usually manual.	Copies of invoices filed in invoice-date sequence.
Periodic Audit	A verification of a file or a phase of processing intended to check for problems and encourage future compliance with control procedures.	The Accounts Receivable Department confirms all of its accounts every June 30.
Redundant Processing	A repetition of processing and an accompanying comparison of individual results for equality.	A second payroll clerk recalculates each gross pay multiplication.
Summary Processing	A redundant process using a summarized amount. This is compared for equality with a control total from the processing of the detailed items.	Total straight-line depreciation can be calculated for each asset class (where everything in an individual class has the same useful life). This balance is compared to total net book value of the property file.
Labeling	The external or internal identificaion of transaction batches or files according to source, application, date, or other identifying characteristics.	See Figure 7.1.
Trailer Record	A record providing a control total for comparison with accumulated counts or values of records processed.	The trailer record indicates 373 blocks, which agrees with the actual count.

CORRECTIVE CONTROLS	EXPLANATION	EXAMPLE
Discrepancy Reports	A listing of items which have violated some detective control and require further investigation.	Each month, a list of delinquent accounts is sent to the Credit Department.
Transaction Trail (Audit Trail)	The availability of a manual or machine-readable means for tracing the status and contents of an individual transaction record backward or forward, between output, processing, and source.	A list of property additions and retirements supports changes to the property file.
Error-Source Statistics	Accumulation of information on type of error and origin. This is used to determine the nature of remedial training needed to reduce the number of errors.	The Keypunch Department keeps track of the number made by each operator and detected by key verification.
Automated Error Correction	Automatic error correction of transactions or records which violate a detective control.	A debit memo is automatically produced and sent to vendors whose invoices exceed purchase order terms.
Upstream Resubmission	The resubmission of corrected error transactions so that they pass through all or more of the detective controls than are exercised over normal transactions (e.g., before input editing).	All rejected inputs are resubmitted the next day after correction as if they were new inputs.
Backup and Recovery	The ability to recreate current master files using appropriate prior master records and transactions.	Prior day's master files and transactions are retained in case the current master file is destroyed.

APPENDIX D

CORPORATE DATA SECURITY
POLICY—THE HARTFORD[1]

[1]Reprinted with permission from The Hartford Insurance Group, July 14, 1982.

Vice President

Hartford Plaza
Hartford, Connecticut 06115

October 31, 1979

ALL HOME OFFICE OFFICERS

In March of this year a memorandum to all Home Office Officers announced that the Data Processing Department had the responsibility to establish and coordinate all data security requirements on a corporate-wide basis, that a security function had been established in the Data Processing Staff Services Department, and that they would, in conjunction with Internal Audit, be developing and coordinating data security policies and procedures.

Attached is the data security policy developed by Data Processing and Internal Audit, which has been reviewed by selected user department senior management. While that review surfaced no substantive disagreement with the policy's content, there was concern raised by the reviewers that the policy's implementation be guided by a committee of user representatives. Formation of such a committee will now commence, concurrent with the publication of the policy.

The policy assigns responsibilities not only to the Data Processing security function for the establishment of standards, procedures, and guidelines in support of this policy, and to the managers of Data Processing functions for their custodial care of data, but also establishes the role and attendant responsibilities of the data owner.

Your support of and proper dissemination of the policy will be appreciated.

Hartford Plaza
Hartford, Connecticut 06115

THE HARTFORD

DATA SECURITY POLICY

I. *Statement of Policy*
   A. *General Responsibility*
       The Hartford Insurance Group Data Processing Department has responsibility for the establishment and coordination of all data security requirements on a corporate-wide basis.
   B. *Data Security Safeguards*
       1. Data shall be processed in a secure environment. The cost of security should be commensurate with the value of the data, considering value to both the data owner and a potential intruder.
       2. Measures with respect to the processing of data will be taken to ensure against the unauthorized modification, destruction, or disclosure of data, whether accidental or intentional. Safeguards will be established to ensure integrity and accuracy of vital company data.
   C. *Scope*
       1. This policy applies to all data maintained or created within the jurisdiction of the data processing functions of The Hartford Insurance Group. This includes, but is not limited to, data maintained or created within:
           a. The Hartford Insurance Group Data Processing Department.
           b. The Data Processing Department of any subsidiary unit.
           c. Satellite data processing installations within the corporation, i.e., users with their own processors and equipment who may or may not interact directly with The Hartford Insurance Group Processing Department or with the Data Processing Department of any subsidiary unit.
           d. Computational Users, i.e., Departments which interact with data processing resources, usually through time-sharing.
           e. Service bureaus which process data for any Hartford Insurance Group Department.
       2. This policy further applies to all applications or operating system data regardless of processing mode. This includes but is not limited to:
           a. Batch, remote, timesharing, or distributed processing.
           b. Applications software and data sets.
           c. Operating systems software, data sets, libraries, or utility programs.
       3. This policy applies solely to computerized data processing activities and not to manually maintained files; further, it applies to data only while in the custodial care of a data processing function.
   D. *Adequacy Standard*
       This policy, and all supporting standards, procedures, and guidelines issued in support of the policy, shall serve as an adequacy standard for data security safeguards; i.e., the basis on which audits will be conducted.

II. *Responsibilities*
  A. *Data Processing Security Function*
    1. The Data Processing security function within the Data Processing Staff Services Department shall be responsible for implementing this policy.
    2. The security function shall establish such standards, procedures, and guidelines as may be necessary to ensure data security in all areas within the jurisdiction of the data processing functions of The Hartford Insurance Group.
    3. The security function shall serve as a mechanism for ongoing review of data security considerations, in the light of technical, environmental, or statutory changes that may arise. It is expected to have an active consultative/review role in all matters impacting data security.
    4. The security function shall provide the necessary support to the data owner and custodian in the performance of their responsibilities.
  B. *Data Owner*
    1. Legal direction such as expressed in the Foreign Corrupt Practices Act, and sound business practice, hold the owner of data responsible for its control. All data within the scope of this policy must have an identified owner; procedures will be established to identify the owner of data.
    2. The data owner has responsibility for specifying data control requirements to the manager with custodial responsibility of data. The owner may relinquish control to the custodian of data only after reasonably evaluating the attendant risk to the data.
  C. *Custodian of Data*
    1. The Manager of each of the various facilities listed in paragraph I-C-1 above has custodial responsibility of data. The Manager will assume responsibility for controlled use of data in the care of his facility.
    2. The jurisdiction of the Manager with custodial responsibility of data begins when data is physically accepted within an established perimeter by his department. Mutually agreed upon standing procedures will define responsibility at the perimeter where exchange of data or information takes place.
  D. *Internal Audit*
    The Internal Audit Department will assist all departments to achieve effective and efficient administration of their respective areas of responsibility.

APPENDIX E

INTERNAL SECURITY

DOCUMENTATION, SPAN PROJECT[1]

DIRECTIONAL STATEMENT FOR THE HWDC DATA
SECURITY POLICY (PAC APPROVED, 08-06-81)

Responsibility for the security of data processed by the Health and Welfare Agency Data Center (HWDC) can logically be separated into two major areas. First, HWDC the provider of computing and related services, and second, the user groups requiring computer services. The user groups would include the program manager, the data collectors, the users of the data and the system development and maintenance organizations.

The Agency's data will be processed in a secure environment. The cost of security, including the testing of security plans and safeguards, should be commensurate with the value of the data, considering value to the data owner/user, the data subject and the potential data abuser.

Measures with respect to the processing of data will be taken to ensure against the unauthorized modification, destruction, or disclosure of data, whether accidental or intentional. Safeguards will be established to ensure integrity and accuracy of vital Agency data.

---

[1]Internal security planning documentation, SPAN Project, Department of Social Services, State of California, principal authors Tom Adams and Mike Grey

The definitions and guidelines contained in the State Administrative Manual (SAM) Section 4842 on EDP Confidentiality and Security were used in formulating this policy. SAM is further a source document for assessing the extent to which safeguards are to be provided.

The responsibility for data security, as shared by the Data Center and the User, are described below.

A. Data Center (HWDC)

The HWDC as the provider of computer and related services shall conduct a comprehensive risk analysis and use it as a basis for determining the safeguards required to provide adequate physical protection of assets such as employees, facilities, and equipment. This physical protection provides the umbrella under which data or information relating to State business can be adequately secured during processing. The HWDC is responsible for:

a. Providing physical security for data and resources in its custody;
b. Providing logical security features for protecting data resources;
c. Providing security for control software and its associated data;
d. Informing the Users System Development and Maintenance Organization of the availability, capabilities, and weakness of security features;
e. Informing the Users System Development and Maintenance Organization of any changes in hardware, control software, or other features which affect data security.
f. Reporting in a timely manner any detected unauthorized actions affecting the Users' data, to the program manager or his/her designee;
g. Developing, maintaining, and testing a disaster recovery plan for the facilities, including hardware and system software;
h. Coordinating with PAC, upon the occurrence of a disaster, the use and sharing of identified available resources on behalf of the entire User community.

B. User

The HWDC Users are identified as those groups requiring computer services and can be further divided into two areas. The Program

Manager, owner/user which also includes the collecters and users of the data, and the System Development group that provides the development, implementation, and maintenance of application systems.

1. Program Manager(Owner/User). The owner/user is responsible for:
   a. Providing physical security for data and resources in its custody;
   b. Providing logical security features for protecting data resources;
   c. Identifying and classifying sensitive data;
   d. Identifying authorized users of the data;
   e. Identifying the risk associated with the data;
   f. Ensuring that measures are implemented by the Data Center, system developers, data collectors, and users of data, to provide the required level of data security;
   g. Developing, maintaining and testing a contingency plan for alternate procedures following a disaster, including manual processing.

2. System Development and Maintenance Organization. The data processing organization, while developing data processing application systems for maintaining data for the program manager, is responsible for:
   a. Providing physical security for data and resources in its custody;
   b. Providing logical security features for protecting data resources;
   c. Developing, maintaining and testing a backup and recovery plan for application systems and data files following a disaster;
   d. Assisting the program manager in developing and testing the contingency plan for alternate procedures following a disaster;
   e. Working with the data center in developing a mutually acceptable plan for testing the facilities disaster recovery plan;
   f. Developing and testing safeguards for application systems;
   g. Including data security requirements in feasibility studies;
   h. Providing adequate control over access to sensitive data and resources in its custody.

SPAN STANDARD PRACTICE #A-18 (POLICIES AND PROCEDURES[2]), DATA SECURITY PLANNING[3]

Special Instructions

This Standard Practice applies to all SPAN staff and is the required ("official") methodology for implementing the appropriate data security safeguards/controls for SPAN.

Purpose

The purpose of the Data Security Planning is to ensure that appropriate action is taken to protect sensitive data from accidental or intentional destruction, modification, or disclosure.

Policy

1. The Management Planning Bureau, through the SPAN Project Security Planner, has the responsibility to (a) provide the planning and leadership to develop a comprehensive system security plan for SPAN; and (b) assemble the SPAN Data Security Controls Inventory.

2. SPAN Bureau Managers have the responsibility to (a) support the Project Security Planner in developing a comprehensive computer system security plan for SPAN; and (b) to implement those safeguards/controls for which they have been identified as having responsibility (Management Planning Bureau is included in this charge relative to error, fraud and system abuse detection).

3. The Management Planning Bureau, through its product/services evaluation function, has the responsibility to give management assurance through periodic quality assurance reports that the SPAN Data Security Controls Inventory is performing to expected standards.

4. The Management Planning Bureau, through its Error, Fraud, and System Abuse Detection function, has the responsibility to monitor all SPAN Operations for possible data security breaches not heretofore recognized by existing controls.

[2]*Management policy*: A continuing directive that applies to recurring questions and problems of concern to an organization as a whole in achieving its objectives. *Procedure*: A standard method of performing specified work.

[3]Administrative Standard Practice #A-18, 12-10-81 Revision: 0.

Procedures

The Data Security Planning Process Data Flow, Figure 1, illustrates the processes covered by this Standard Practice.

1.0 *Determine Data Security Safeguards Controls*—This process is the specific responsibility of the SPAN Project Security Planner. This process will be conducted by applying the SPAN Data Security Design & Control Methodology illustrated in the Data Flow, Figure 2. The methodology package is attached. The product of this process is the SPAN Data Security Controls Inventory. The Inventory consists of the inventory of safeguards in the SPAN system, a description of the safeguard, and the organization responsible for

Span Data Security Planning Process

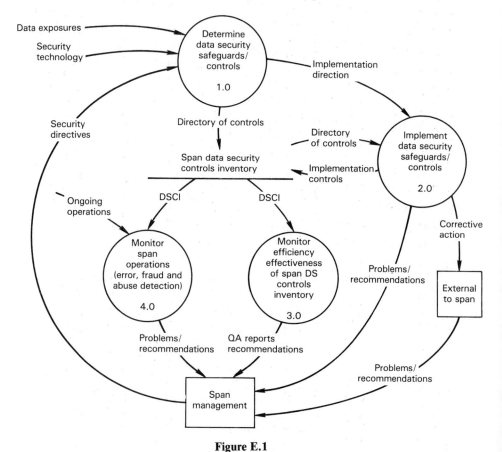

Figure E.1

development and maintenance, operations, output analysis and corrective action.

2.0 *Implement Data Security Safeguards/Controls*—The implementation process can be subdivided into Development, Installation, Operations, Output Analysis and Corrective Action for each safeguard. The organization responsible for each of these functions by safeguard, will be identified in Process 1.0.

3.0 *Monitor Efficiency & Effectiveness of SPAN Data Security Controls Inventory*—This process is the specific responsibility of the product/services evaluation function within the Management Planning Bureau. Periodic Quality Assurance reports will be prepared reporting on the performance of specific safeguards identified in the SPAN Data Security Controls Inventory.

4.0 *Monitor SPAN Operations*—This process is the specific responsibility of the Error, Fraud, and System Abuse Detection function within the Management Planning Bureau.

MANAGEMENT PLANNING BUREAU REPORT ON SPAN SECURITY PLANNING[4]

Overview

Security is too big, too complex, and too specialized for any one organization to have full responsibility on a project the size of SPAN.

However, someone needs to be responsible for tying all the pieces together, and this rests within the SPAN Management Planning organization. The SPAN FSR reads: "This function (Management Planning) will provide the planning and task force leadership to develop a comprehensive computer system security plan for SPAN." (FSR pg. I-12)

The overall strategy for accomplishing this objective is to approach the security issue from these four (4) perspectives:

1. Determine the appropriate Data Security Safeguards/Controls.
2. Implement the identified Data Security Safeguards/Controls.
3. Monitor the Efficiency and Effectiveness of the SPAN Data Security Safeguards/Controls.
4. Monitor the SPAN Operations.

[4]04-14-82; Rev. 0; File Ref. 4.1/8.1.6.1.

The first perspective, (1) to *determine* (identify and assign responsibility) the appropriate controls, is the objective of the SPAN Data Security Design and Control Methodology, and the subject of the remainder of this report.

The second perspective, (2) to *implement* the control, is the responsibility of the operating organization in DSS (not the Management Planning organization).

The third perspective, (3) to *monitor* the performance of the implemented control, is a special form of quality assurance reporting.

The fourth perspective, (4) to *monitor* the SPAN operations, looking for security breaches, problems, etc. *even with* the presence of the implemented controls, is the role of a special detection group (Error, Fraud and System Abuse); a complementary unit to planning and quality assurance in the Management Planning organization.

These concepts are incorporated in SPAN Standard Practice #A-18, DATA SECURITY PLANNING.

DATA SECURITY DESIGN AND CONTROL METHODOLOGY

The Data Security Design and Control Methodology was established to aid in the process of identifying the most cost effective system security safeguards. The intent was to develop and describe a generic methodology which would be applicable to most data processing based systems or processes requiring security controls.

The methodology consists of twelve (12) separate sequential steps. A description of each step and a diagram follow.

1. *Identify System Data Exposure Control Points.* The purpose of identifying the Data Exposure Control Points (DECP) is to locate all possible exposures of the data as it is processed through the system.

2. *Identify Data Exposures.* The purpose of this process is to identify the data exposures, by exposure type, at all Data Exposure Control Points within the system.

3. *Map Data Exposures to Control Points.* The purpose of mapping the data exposures to the control points is to combine and link possible associated exposures and reflect total exposure by control point.

Data Security
Design and Control Methodology

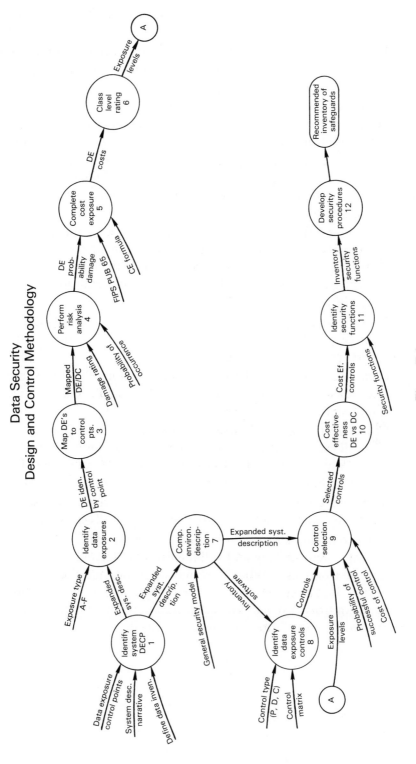

Figure E.2

4. *Perform Risk Analysis.* The purpose of this step is to establish the dollar value if the data exposure occurs and the probability or likelihood of such data exposure occurring.

5. *Complete Cost Exposure.* The purpose of this step is to establish the annual cost exposure using the probability of occurrence and the amount of damage established in the Risk Analysis (Step 4).

6. *Class Level Rating.* The purpose of this process is to rank the identified data exposures by dollar value per year within Data Exposure Control Points and then give a class level rating to all identified data exposures.

7. *Computer Environment Description.* The purpose of this process is to identify within the computer environment (of the System Workflow Description developed in Step 1) the internal interfaces that can be equated to Data Exposure Control Points as data is processed internally.

8. *Identify Data Exposure Controls.* The purpose of this process is to identify an inventory of possible controls and type these controls by Preventive, Detective, or Corrective.

9. *Control Set Selection.* This step is the selection of controls to protect the data integrity during the identified data exposures and/or eliminate the data exposures.

10. *Cost Effectiveness of Data Exposures Versus Data Controls.* This step will calculate the cost effectiveness of the control sets selected in Step 9 by comparing the Ranked Annualized Cost of Data Exposure (Step 6) against the estimated costs of Data Control (Step 9).

11. *Identify Security Functions.* This process will identify the security function(s) that the selected cost effective control sets will perform.

12. *Develop Security Procedures.* This process is the final step of the Security Methodology and will identify the Recommended Inventory of Controls. "What" products will provide these controls. "Who" is responsible for the development and implementation of these controls. "When" the controls will be developed and implemented. "Where" the controls are defined.

CONTACTS

Name	Phone/MS	Subject Areas
Tom Adams	924-2905 MS 19-45	SPAN Security Program, Organizations, Overview, etc.
Mike Grey	924-2977 MS 19-45	Data Security Design and Control Methodology, Field Tests, Applications
Kathy Porter	924-2974 MS 19-45	Security Reference Material
Tony DeMaio	924-2994 MS 19-45	Error, Fraud and System Abuse Detection Methodologies
Bill Nidever	924-2976 MS 19-45	Quality Assurance on Data Security related Standard Practice and Procedures

REFERENCES

A. Data Security Planning, SPAN Standard Practice #A-18, dated 12-10-81.
B. MPB Report on Fraud Detection—California, dated 01-27-82.
C. MPB Report on Organizational Involvement in Security, dated 01-27-82.

APPENDIX F

DP ASSET PROTECTION

SELF-ASSESSMENT

GUIDE—IBM CORPORATION[1]

INTRODUCTION AND INSTRUCTIONS

Purpose

The purpose of the Data Processing Asset Protection Self-Assessment Guide is to:

- Help line management understand and fulfill its DP asset protection responsibilities—as defined in Corporate Instruction and in divisional and site instructions that have been issued on this same subject.
- Improve our overall data processing asset protection posture:
  - by identifying and correcting *basic* data processing asset protection exposures
  - by helping line management identify and better protect *key data processing assets*
  - by identifying improvements needed in our operational environment, procedures, and products.
- Have the annual self-assessments required by CI 2-109A conducted in a consistent manner throughout the entire division.

[1]Reproduced with permission IBM Corporation.

Scope

This Guide has been designed for use by all Line Managers supplying and/or using data processing services, *and* by all owners and custodians of Data Processing Assets, e.g., terminals, mini-computers, programs, systems, data files, etc.

How to Use This Guide

Familiarize yourself with Corporate Instruction and division and site instructions or operating procedures relevant to the protection of data processing assets. Then complete the "General Assessment" section of this package *and all other applicable sections.*

In answering the questions check the *yes, no,* or *not applicable* columns and provide comments as appropriate.

Refer to CI as necessary. (The letters and numbers (e.g., D1, D2, etc.) following most of the questions are references to sections and subsections of CI.)

All *no* answers should have comments and must be addressed in corrective Action Plans or Risk Acceptance Documentation.

After answering all appropriate questions, summarize your findings on the "Assessment Summary," then follow the instructions provided by your Site Security Manager about how to prepare Action Plans and Risk Management Documentation. (These will generally be functional, rather than departmental documents, and will detail each exposure or compliance problem, the actions planned, checkpoint dates, the responsible manager, etc.—or a risk management position explaining why no corrective action will be taken.)

Your completed self-assessment guide is subject to audit so it is in your own best interest to perform the assessment thoroughly. The results will be reflected in the division's *Operating Plans.*

If you need help while conducting the assessment, contact your site's Security Manager or DP Security Administrator.)

Assessment Guide—Contents

This package contains the following:

- Cover page
- Introduction/Instruction Section
- Self-Assessment Questionnaires entitled:

- General Assessment
- Owner (of DP Assets) Assessment
- User (of DP Assets) Assessment
- Custodian (supplier of DP Services) Assessment
- Assessment Summary
- Attachments A/B

DP ASSET PROTECTION — SELF ASSESSMENT: GENERAL ASSESSMENT

CONFIDENTIAL (when completed)

Instructions

- Read the instructions shown on the preceding page.
- Answer all of the questions listed below. (These questions apply to almost all owners, users, and custodians of data processing assets.)
- Complete other questionnaires, as applicable.

	Yes	No	NA	Comments
BASIC DP ASSET PROTECTION RESPONSIBILITIES				
1. Have you and the appropriate people in your organization been familiarized with Corporate Instruction and divisional and site instructions relevant to the classification and control of IBM data processing assets?				
2. Do you and your people understand your DP Asset Protection responsibilities? B2–B6				
3. Do you understand the *Selective Protection of Asset Program*?				
4. Have you established procedures to assure the proper classification and control of all data processing assets (e.g., hardware, computer input and output, programs, and data files) originated by the personnel in your organization? B2–B6, D1–D7				
5. Have you identified your organization's key data processing assets? If so, are they adequately protected?				

	Yes	No	N/A	Comments
6. If you or your people work with data processing information originated (owned) by other organizations, is all of that information, in your opinion, properly classified and controlled? B3				
7. Are you and your people currently fulfilling your *other* DP Asset Protection responsibilities? B2–B5				
8. Have you conducted previous assessments of your DP asset protection posture? If so, have you corrected the exposures identified by those assessments? B6				

*SOFTWARE AND DATA CONTROL

	Yes	No	N/A	Comments
9. Is access to Confidential and/or Registered Confidential (RIC) data processing information limited to those individuals authorized by its owner? D1				
10. Is destruction of classified material including carbon paper and microfiche done by burning, grinding or other suitable methods? E11				
11. Are nonregular employees (i.e., subcontract, part time, temporary) permitted to access classified information? D1 If so, are nondisclosure agreements in force?				

*CRYPTOGRAPHY

	Yes	No	N/A	Comments
12. If you have information that is required by IBM standards to be encrypted, is it encrypted? D1, F1				
13. Cryptography is not to be used as a primary method of controlling system access to data. Do you comply? F1				

*TERMINALS/COMPUTING INSTALLATIONS AND SUPPORTING FACILITIES

	Yes	No	N/A	Comments
**14. Are all terminals under IBM management control, e.g., located on owned or leased premises, used only for business, etc.? I1–I3				
**15. Have terminal users been instructed that terminals are only to be used when under IBM management control? I1–I3				
16. Are telephone numbers used to access Internal Data Processing systems treated by you and your people as Internal Use Only information? D5 Are these numbers excluded from publication in telephone listings or directories? D5				

	Yes	No	NA	Comments
*TERMINALS/COMPUTING INSTALLATIONS AND SUPPORTING FACILITIES (cont.)				
**17. Have you informed your people that Internal DP Equipment is to be used for Business Purposes only? B2, B5, G1 Do you periodically check your people for compliance?				
**18. Do you minimize the possibility of *unauthorized* personnel using your terminals, mini-computers and other DP Equipment? B2, I2, I3				
MESSAGES AND TEXT				
19. If you have a sending, forwarding or receiving station for messages and text (i.e., ITPS, facsimile, wideband, etc.), do you comply with the requirements in Section J?				
RECORDS				
20. Can you demonstrate to an auditor through record-keeping or other techniques that you are meeting the requirements? C, K				

*Denotes that additional questions on these and other topics appear in other Questionnaires within this Self-Assessment Guide—complete those Questionnaires, as appropriate.

**Denotes that in addition to the referenced sections of CI you should also read Security Instructions D-1A, and D-1B or their site equivalents.

DP ASSET PROTECTION SELF ASSESSMENT: OWNER (OF DP ASSETS) ASSESSMENT

CONFIDENTIAL (when completed)

Instructions

Answer the questions listed below only if:

- You have completed the "General Assessment" questionnaire.
- You are the Owner of data processing assets as defined in Section B3 of Corporate Instruction.

	Yes	No	NA	Comments

SOFTWARE AND DATA CONTROL

1. If data processing equipment is used to create or maintain Registered Confidential (RIC) information, is the Site RIC Recorder aware of, and controlling, its reproduction and distribution (including transmission?) D1

2. Are records of access to, custody change, declassification and disposal of RIC information in a DP environment provided to and maintained by the Recorder? D1

3. Are all of your developed application programs classified *at least* Internal Use only? D3

4. Is all of the associated program documentation (e.g., punched cards, tapes, magnetic cards, diskettes, cassettes, microfiche) marked with the appropriate security classification and control statement? D3

5. Is the appropriate classification and control statement imbedded in all forms of software? D3

6. If you own any sensitive programs, control elements and restricted utilities, has DP installation management been made aware of them, i.e., are they on a control list? D6, D7

7. Are there written procedures for sensitive programs, control elements and restricted utilities which describe overall control strategy, emergency procedures, and provisions for protection in back-up and off-site storage situations? D6, D7

8. Are controlled files of specifications and changes kept for all sensitive programs, control elements and restricted utilities? D6, D7

9. Are changes to sensitive programs documented, approved by owner management, and verified by independent review? D6

10. Are software modules and associated program documentation internally marked as prescribed for a sensitive program? D6

11. Is the update of production software for sensitive programs, control elements and restricted utilities approved by programming and installation management? D6, D7

12. Is authorization by management required for reproduction or introduction of sensitive programs, control elements and restricted utilities? D6, D7

	Yes	No	NA	Comments
SOFTWARE AND DATA CONTROL (cont.)				
13. Are all associated displays or print-outs obtained by restricted utilities treated at the same classification level as the data being accessed? D7				
14. With the controls now being used, would collusion between two or more employees be necessary to modify a sensitive program without detection?				
APPLICATION DESIGN AND REVIEW				
15. Are all internal data processing applications under development or enhancement reviewed for compliance and approved before promotion to operational status? E1				
16. Are all operational data processing applications reviewed during self-assessment? E1				
17. Has the ownership of all applications, software, and data been assigned by management? E2				
18. Have you classified input, output, data, and software, and informed the custodian as appropriate? E2				
19. Have you designated sensitive programs, restricted utilities, and control elements, and informed the custodian as appropriate? E2				
20. Have you specified appropriate business and asset protection controls for your information (data files, etc.), and informed those with a need to know? Do you monitor compliance? E2, E3, E4, E6, B3				
21. Have you done an annual review of the security classification and the control of your information? E2				
22. Do you have access controls for Confidential and RIC information? E2				
23. Are the business controls defined in section E4 of CI in place and working? E4				
24. If the data processing system used for your information has the facility to control update of software and data by read, update, and/or execute authority, do you use it or require others to use it?				
25. Following log-on to DP systems is access to classified data controlled on the basis of previously validated user identification? E7				

	Yes	No	N/A	Comments
26. Information password protection or encryption is to be used as an alternative or as a supplement to the preferred access control method. Is it? E7				
27. Is unencrypted RIC information or unencrypted sensitive programs erased on storage devices (i.e., tapes, disks, memory, etc.) prior to reuse? E8				
28. Does your application system or program erase other classified unencrypted residual information prior to disposal or nonuse? If not, does the custodian do it? E8				
29. Is information classified higher than Internal Use Only used for testing only under authorized and supervised conditions? E9				
30. Does the appropriate security classification and control statement appear on all applicable computer inputs and terminal displays, printouts, and is it imbedded in tapes and disks, etc.? E10				
31. Is classified information encrypted as required by CI? D1, E10, J2				
32. Is the classification associated with the encrypted text apparent at the time of decryption? E10				
33. Are classification and control statements visible without enlargement? E11				
34. Are reports of accesses to RIC information and sensitive programs created as required by 2-109A? (Twice monthly for RIC, monthly for sensitive programs.) E12				
35. Is an individual assigned to react to access violations? E13				
36. If so, are the reports analyzed and timely investigations done? E12				
37. If information is password protected, is the password nonobvious and nontrivial? E16				
38. If your people have disclosed passwords to others, have you or the system administrator been made aware of the disclosure? E16 Do you approve the disclosure?				
39. Are information access passwords changed promptly when individuals no longer have the "need to know"? E16				
40. Are information passwords changed at least every six months? E16				

	Yes	No	N/A	Comments
CRYPTOGRAPHY				
41. If you use an encryption facility other than one provided by Information Systems Management it must be compatible with the encryption facility used in the product program. Is it? F1				
42. Do you keep clear text back-up until the encryption key has been validated? F2				
43. Are your encryption keys recorded and properly classified with at least the classification of the clear text? F2, F4				
44. Do your encryption keys conform to requirements stated in CI? F3				
45. When transferring encrypted information, are your keys communicated separately and securely? F4				
46. Is all RIC encryption key custody, disclosure, declassification, and disposal reported to the Recorder twice monthly? F4				

DP ASSET PROTECTION SELF ASSESSMENT: CUSTODIAN (SUPPLIER OF DP SERVICES) ASSESSMENT

CONFIDENTIAL (when completed)

Instructions

Answer the questions listed below only if:

- You have completed the "General Assessment" questionnaire.
- You are the Custodian of data processing assets as defined in Section B4 of Corporate Instruction.

	Yes	No	NA	Comments

SOFTWARE AND DATA CONTROL

1. If data processing equipment is used to create or maintain Registered Confidential (RIC) information, is the site RIC Recorder aware of, and controlling, its reproduction and distribution (including transmission?) D1

2. Are records of access to, custody change, declassification and disposal of RIC information in a DP environment provided to and maintained by the Recorder? D1

3. Does the Recorder handle the decontrol of Registered Confidential tapes, disks, etc.? D1

*4. Are appropriate controls in place to protect classified output, including reports, data and software, through delivery to the end user? D2

5. Is your program documentation (e.g., punched cards, tapes, magnetic cards, diskettes, cassettes, microfiche) marked with the appropriate security classification and control statements? D3

6. Are tapes, disks, etc. marked with the highest classification of data contained therein? D4

7. Are there written procedures for sensitive programs, control elements and restricted utilities which describe overall control strategy, emergency procedures, and provisions for protection in back-up and off-site storage situations? D6, D7

8. Are controlled files of specifications and changes kept for all sensitive programs, control elements and restricted utilities? D6, D7

9. Are changes to sensitive programs documented, approved by owner management, and verified by independent review? D6

10. Are sensitive programs, control elements and restricted utilities access controlled, either by software or procedures? D6, D7

11. Is the authorization for update of production sensitive programs, control elements and restricted utilities approved by appropriate programming and installation management? D6, D7

12. Is there separation of duties so that a programmer can access a sensitive program only for authorized purposes? D6

	Yes	No	N/A	Comments
SOFTWARE AND DATA CONTROL (cont.)				
13. Is authorization by appropriate management required for reproduction or introduction of sensitive programs, control elements and restricted utilities? D6, D7				
14. Are owners provided with monthly reports of access activity for sensitive programs? D6				
15. If you own any sensitive programs, control elements and restricted utilities, has appropriate management been made aware of them, i.e., are they on a control list? D6, D7				
16. Are there written procedures for sensitive programs, control elements and restricted utilities which describe overall control strategy, emergency procedures, and provisions for protection in back-up and off-site storage situations? D6, D7				
17. Are sensitive programs, control elements and restricted utilities controlled to allow access only to authorized persons doing authorized work? D6, D7				
18. Are all internal data processing applications under development or enhancement reviewed for compliance with and approved before promotion to operational status? E1				
19. Are the owners of all common applications identifiable and have they communicated business and asset protection control requirements to you? E3				
20. Are business controls defined in Section E4 of CI in place and working?				
21. If the data processing system used for your information has the facility to control update of software and data by read, update, and/or execute authority, do you use it or require others to use it?				
22. Is unencrypted RIC information or unencrypted sensitive programs erased on storage devices (i.e., tapes, disks, memory, etc.) prior to reuse? E8				
23. Is unencrypted Confidential information erased prior to removal from inventory or from the restricted access area? E8				
24. Is other classified unencrypted residual information erased prior to disposal or non-IBM use? E8				
25. Is disposal of unencrypted RIC information reported twice monthly to the recorder? E8				

	Yes	No	NA	Comments
26. Does the appropriate security classification and control statement appear on all applicable computer inputs, terminal displays and printouts, and is it imbedded in tapes and disks, etc.? E10				
27. Are classification and control statements visible without enlargement? E11				
28. Are reports of accesses to RIC information and custody change activity reported twice monthly to the recorder? E12				
29. Are sensitive program activity reports provided to owners and appropriate installation management on a monthly basis? E12				
30. Are reports of RIC and sensitive program activities analyzed and timely investigations conducted? E12 Has an individual been assigned the Investigation Responsibility? E13				
31. Is there detection and reporting of unauthorized attempts to gain computer, software, and data access? E13				
32. Has an individual been assigned to investigate the above violations? E13 Are they done in a timely manner?				
33. Are user and job identification codes traceable to the user for the lifetime of the records and reports? E14				
34. If you are the custodian of a system having centralized logon password controls, are passwords of required length, randomly selected, not obvious or trivial, classified at least IBM Confidential, and changed at least every 2 months? E15				

CRYPTOGRAPHY

	Yes	No	NA	Comments
35. If you use or provide an encryption facility is it compatible with the Program Product? F1				
36. Do you maintain and back-up all versions of cryptographic hardware and software—in order to convert back level or archived encrypted data to clear text? F2				
37. When transferring encrypted information, are your keys communicated separately and securely? F4				
38. Is all RIC encryption key custody, disclosure, declassification, and disposal reported to the Recorder twice monthly? F4				

	Yes	No	NA	Comments

COMPUTING INSTALLATIONS AND
SUPPORTING FACILITIES

39. Have you been fully informed of the controls required for the protection of assets in your custody? G1

40. Have you effectively informed the users of your services and the owners of data and data processing applications of:
    (a) The system security facilities and administrative procedures available to protect classified DP assets—and of how to use them? G1
    (b) Recommended protection practices? G1
    (c) Installation restrictions, e.g., what they must do to meet unique installation security requirements? G1

41. Are users frequently and effectively informed that services and resources are to be used for business purposes only? G1

42. Computing equipment and supporting facilities must be located within restricted access areas if continued operation is vital or if classified information is processed on the equipment. Are they? G2

43. Are supporting telecommunications facilities such as telephone closets, wire rooms, and frame rooms, administered as separate areas of restricted physical access? G2

44. Are measures taken to prevent and detect attempts to disrupt operations or to enter or leave the restricted area in an unauthorized manner? G2

45. Is routine physical access limited to those persons whose work stations are within the restricted access area, and discouraged after scheduled working hours? G2

46. Does each person in the installation wear visible identification as a visitor or employee? G3

47. Are all visitor entries and all nonroutine entries of regular personnel logged? Is this log presented to appropriate management for review and follow-up? G3

48. When users and authorized support personnel are permitted within restricted access areas they must be under observation and control. Are they? G3

	Yes	No	N/A	Comments
49. Are other visitors escorted while within the restricted access areas? G3				
50. Is classified information within the installation properly identified, protected, and released only to authorized users or its owner? G4				
51. Are controls in place to detect and deter unauthorized attempts to access or remove classified information? Is responsibility clearly assigned for timely and effective response to such attempts? G4				
52. Is classified carbon paper, overrun copies, and other classified waste properly controlled and disposed of? G4				
53. Does your installation comply with Corporate Facilities Practice? G5				
54. Has the computer room been constructed using noncombustible material? G5				
55. Have card and paper storage rooms been constructed using noncombustible material and are they sprinkler protected? G5				
CONTROL OF VOLUMES (e.g., tapes, disk packs, etc.)				
56. Are external labels which reflect security classifications affixed to all tapes, disks, etc., containing classified information? H1				
57. Are classified tapes, disks, etc. controlled to prevent unauthorized access to classified information? H1				
58. Is access controlled according to classifications? H1 —during mounting/demounting? —during transmission/possession/transport? —while in storage?				
59. Are procedures in place for classification and reclassification of tapes, disks, etc.? H1				
60. Is someone assigned the responsibility for the control of classified tapes, disks, etc.? H1 —during off shift? —during nonregular operations?				
61. Are record keeping and inventory controls in place for all tapes, disks, etc.? H2				
62. Do you have a record keeping system that uniquely identifies and accounts for every tape, disk, etc.? H2				
63. Is someone designated to control the tapes, disks, etc.? H2				

	Yes	No	NA	Comments
CONTROL OF VOLUMES (cont.)				
64. Do you have inventory control procedures for all volumes? H2 Are inventories taken as often as required? H2				
65. Are there special controls, procedures and personnel responsibility assignments for RIC volumes? H2 —for storage? —for handling? —for possession? —for transport? —for transmission? —for declassification/disposal?				
66. Are the procedures for removal of volumes from the restricted access area adequate? H3				
67. Is the tape, disk, etc. storage area in compliance with Corporate Facilities Practice? G5, H4				
68. Has someone been assigned to review the volume storage rooms for compliance with CFP and to take corrective action, if required? H4				

*Denotes that in addition to the referenced sections of CI you should also read Security Instruction D-1C.

DP ASSET PROTECTION SELF ASSESSMENT: USER (OF DP ASSETS) ASSESSMENT

CONFIDENTIAL (when completed)

Instructions

Answer the questions listed below only if:

- You or your manager have completed the "General Assessment" questionnaire. (You should at least review its content with him before proceeding.)
- You are the *User* of data processing assets as defined in Section B2 of Corporate Instruction.

	Yes	No	N/A	Comments

RESPONSIBILITIES, COMPLIANCE, AND CONTROLS

1. Data processing assets (e.g., data processing equipment, programs, data files, etc.) are to be used only for management approved business purposes. Do you comply? B2

*2. As a user of data processing assets you are required by CI to determine the equipment, programming, and system security facilities and administrative services available to you to protect DP assets. Have you done so and do you use them, as required? B2, C1–C3, D1, D6, E7–E9

3. You must also comply with special business and security controls, if any are required of you by the owners of the DP Assets or the supplier of DP services you use. Do you? B2

APPLICATION, INFORMATION AND SYSTEM CONTROLS

4. If you are the user of a common application is the owner known to you and has he communicated business and asset protection control requirements to you? E3

5. If you are the user of a system that does not have centralized logon password controls, is your password of required length, randomly selected, not obvious or trivial, classified at least Confidential, changed at least every 2 months and not reused more frequently than once every 15 months? E15

6. Are your job identification codes traceable to you for the lifetime of the records and reports? E14

7. Do you prevent accidental or inadvertent disclosure of passwords? E15

8. When using information access passwords, do you treat them as securely as the associated data, i.e., based on its security classification? E16

9. Are information access passwords changed upon termination of the business need of an individual to whom the password is known? E16

10. Are information passwords changed at least every six months? E16

11. If you are also the owner or custodian of DP assets you must also complete other questionnaires included in this guide. Have you?

*You must use appropriate security facilities and/or administrative services to protect the assets even if the owner of the assets has not given you special security instructions relevant to their control.

227

ASSESSMENT SUMMARY

CONFIDENTIAL (when completed)

	Yes	No	N/A	Comments
INSTRUCTIONS: This summary is to be completed by line management and approved as shown below. (1) Has this assessment helped you and your people better understand your data processing asset protection responsibilities? (2) Has it helped you understand how to fulfill them? (3) Has the assessment helped you identify any key data processing assets? (4) If you answered yes to question 3, have you included them in a formal asset protection plan? (5) Will the assessment and your associated action plan and/or risk acceptance documentation, in your opinion, stand the test of an in-depth audit?				

The following assessment questionnaires were applicable to my organization and were completed:

	Question Summary			
	# Asked	# Answered Yes	# Answered No*	# Answered N/A
General Assessment	20			
Owner Assessment	46			
User Assessment	11			
Custodian Assessment	68			
Assessment Summary	5			

*Denotes that all questions answered *NO* are to be addressed in a formal action plan and/or risk acceptance document. Follow the instructions of your Site Security Manager on how to prepare those documents and to have them approved.

Name of Organization Assessed: _____

Assessment Completed By: _____ _____ _____
                          Manager's Signature   Dept.   Date

Assessment Approved By: _____ _____ _____
                         Manager's Signature   Dept.   Date

ATTACHMENT "A"

CONFIDENTIAL (when completed)

**Data Processing Asset Protection: Security
Exposures Committed for Resolution**

___ Custodians of Data Processing Assets
___ Owners and Users of Data Processing Assets
(check one of the above)

The format below is to be used to report all exposures planned for resolution:

Problem name and/or description. _____

Plan to resolve (include checkpoint dates and name of manager responsible for fix). _____

Dependencies/exposures (include any item which may impact resolving problem). _____

If problem has been reported previously, where, when; i.e., ICR Plan, etc. _____

Approval signatures (as required by CI 2-109A).

CONFIDENTIAL (when completed)

Data Processing Asset Protection:
Security Exposures <u>Not Committed</u> for Resolution

___ Custodians of Data Processing Assets
___ Owners and Users of Data Processing Assets
(check one of the above)

The format below is to be used to report all items *not committed* for resolution:

Problem name and/or description.

Resolution alternatives (including manpower and dollars needed).

Reason alternatives unacceptable, e.g., not cost justified.

Recommendation of how the exposure should be resolved.

If problem has been reported previously, where, when; i.e., ICR
Plan, etc.

Approval signatures (as required by CI 2-109A).

GLOSSARY

Ballpark estimate.   An estimate within a specified range.

Chunk.   A portion of a whole system, process, or methodology that can be understood, communicated, or managed.

Data.   Any representation of facts, concepts, or instructions to which meaning is or might be assigned when properly processed by human or automatic means.

Data dictionary.   A centralized repository of information about data such as meaning, relationships to other data, origin, usage, and format.

Data integrity.   Preservation of data for its intended purpose; a quality of data that exists as long as accidental or malicious destruction, alteration or loss of data are prevented.

Destroy.   To render useless or meaningless in any form or context to anyone.

Disaster.   The loss of capability to perform the business function.

Disclose.   To make known or reveal to unauthorized parties.

Evolutionary structuring.   A quick approach to modeling (prototyping an entire system; very rough approximations with later refinement and attention to detail.

Exposure.   The possible result or consequence of adverse actions or events.

Grid.   A tabular form of display (i.e., grate or lattice) used for illustrating meaningful relationships generally in rows and columns.

Hazard.   Potential to inflict harm.

Information.   The meaning an individual assigns to data by means of the conventions applied to that data.

Life cycle.   Period of time from beginning to end.

Matrix.   *See* Grid.

Modify.   To change or alter the original form or qualities.

Monolithic structuring.   A well-ordered and highly-structured procedure dealing with a system as a single, complete entity throughout the development process. Each process step (analysis, design, program, installation) is completely performed sequentially as a separate phase.

Quik.   Emphasized notation of the word quick.

Resource.   An asset; any facility of a system that has value.

Security.   Protection of resources.

System.   A set of operations and procedures through which a business activity is accomplished; a structured combination of interacting parts working together to satisfy a set of objectives or achieve a common goal.

Threat.   Expression of intent to inflict harm; something that could or might happen causing loss of assets or reduction in value of assets.

INDEX